HARVARD BUSINESS ESSENTIALS

Managing Change and Transition

Harvard Business School Press | *Boston, Massachusetts*

12 11 10   10 9

Requests for permission to use or reproduce material from this book should be directed to permissions@hbsp.harvard.edu, or mailed to Permissions, Harvard Business School Publishing, 60 Harvard Way, Boston, Massachusetts 02163.

978-1-57851-874-6 (ISBN 13)

Library of Congress Cataloging-in-Publication Data

Managing change and transition.

p. cm. — (Harvard business essentials series)

Includes bibliographical references and index.

ISBN 1-57851-874-1

1. Organizational change. 2. Organizational change—Management.

I. Series.

HD58.8 .M2544 2003

658.1'6—dc21

2002011668

Contents

Introduction   **1**

1   The Dimensions of Change   **7**
Examining the Different Types and Approaches

   Types of Change   8
   Two Different Approaches to Change   10
   Summing Up   15

2   Are You Change–Ready?   **17**
Preparing for Organizational Change

   Respected and Effective Leaders   18
   Motivation to Change   19
   A Nonhierarchical Organization   24
   Becoming Change-Ready   25
   Summing Up   29

3   Seven Steps to Change   **31**
A Systematic Approach

   The Seven Steps   33
   Roles for Leaders, Managers, and HR   46
   Mistakes to Avoid   47
   Summing Up   49

4   Implementation   **51**
Putting Your Plan in Motion

   Enlist the Support and Involvement of Key People   53
   Craft an Implementation Plan   54
   Support the Plan with Consistent Behaviors and Messages   56
   Develop Enabling Structures   57

Celebrate Milestones   58
Communicate Relentlessly   60
Using Consultants   62
Summing Up   67

5   Social and Human Factors   69
Reactions to Change
The Rank and File   70
The Resisters   74
The Change Agents   77
Summing Up   81

6   Helping People Adapt   83
Strategies to Help Reduce Stress and Anxiety
Reactions to Change: A Sense of Loss and Anxiety   85
Stages in Reaction to Change   86
The Conventional Advice   88
What Individuals Can Do for Themselves   89
How Managers Can Help Employees Cope   92
Rethinking Resisters   96
Summing Up   99

7   Toward Continuous Change   101
Staying Competitive through Change
Continuous Incremental Change   102
Can People Handle It?   104
Getting to Continuous Change   106
Summing Up   110

Appendix A: Useful Implementation Tools   113

**Appendix B: How to Choose and
Work with Consultants   119**

Notes   125
For Further Reading   129
Index   133
About the Subject Adviser   137
About the Writer   138

Managing Change
and Transition

Introduction

Pick any industry and chances are that it looked very different in the 1970s than it did in the 1980s. Likewise, the industries of the 1980s had changed drastically by the succeeding decade. Agribusiness. Air travel. Auto manufacturing. Banking. Biotech. Computers. Electronics. Pharmaceuticals. Steel. Software. Telecommunications. Each of these established industries has passed through one or more wringers over the past several decades. Quality improvement. Adoption of new methods. Adaptation to new technologies. Response to regulatory change. Facing up to new competitors. And most will be forced through a new set of changes in the years ahead.

If the industries themselves have changed so drastically, clearly the companies within them have experienced their own unique upheavals. IBM was adrift and slowly sinking before it was rescued and refitted under new leadership and a core of energetic and determined employees. Microsoft has transformed itself from a software company to an integrator of computer-Internet solutions. General Electric has gone through several successive waves of change over the past twenty-something years. Enron rose like a rocket on its innovative approach to energy trading before overreaching management blew it to bits. These companies represent simply a few episodes in the saga of corporate transformation. Even enterprises as small as your local independent bookstore are changing how they operate. Those that don't change are bound to stagnate or fail.

Although it's impossible to anticipate the when, what, and where of change, it *is* something businesses can count on—and should plan for. Accepting the necessity and inevitability of change enables them to see times of transition not as threats but as opportunities—opportunities for reinventing the company and its culture. Indicators that life at work is about to change include:

- **A merger, acquisition, or divestiture.** Mergers and acquisitions are often the means by which organizations grow. Divestitures are strategic attempts to redirect assets or to focus the organization in some particular direction. Such "restructuring" changes almost always result in duplications of functions, which must be corrected through painful layoffs.

- **The launch of a new product or service.** These connect a company with new customer markets and, often, new competitors. In these cases, adaptation and learning are essential.

- **A new leader.** Change should be expected with the arrival of any new leader. Like a new owner of an old house, a new leader will be tempted to alter or remodel existing business processes. In many cases, this means a substantial turnover among senior executives. The new leader generally doesn't feel comfortable until he is comfortable with all the people around him. Change will cascade down from these new executives.

- **A new technology.** Technology is transforming the world of work. Information technology in particular is changing not just how we work, but when we work and from which locations. Close to 23 percent of the U.S. workforce now does some amount of "telework" from home, from a client location, or from a satellite office. In addition so-called "disruptive" technologies can render a company's products or services obsolete in a very short time. Where are all the "supercomputers" we used to hear about? And who needs travelers' checks in an age of credit cards and ATMs? These are being displaced.

The fact that organizations must undergo continual change does not mean that people enjoy the process, or that the experience of change is pleasant. On the contrary, change is often disheartening and frustrating, and generally leaves a number of casualties in its wake. Managers often complain that change takes too long or that it's too costly. Alternately, some worry that it doesn't last long enough or cost enough to get the job done. People at the bottom claim that the "top" doesn't practice what it preaches. The people at the top grouse that the folks at the bottom are dragging their feet. People in the middle blame everyone else.

Change is almost always disruptive and, at times, traumatic. Because of this, many people avoid it if they can. Nevertheless, change is part of organizational life and essential for progress. Those who know how to anticipate it, catalyze it, and manage it will find their careers, and their companies, more satisfying and successful.

What's Ahead

In this book you will learn how to manage change constructively, and how to help your company, division, and people deal with the upheavals of change. You'll also learn practical things you can do to make change initiatives more successful and less painful for the people you manage.

The literature on change management is large and growing constantly, with dozens of books and case studies published every year. This book compiles the best information on this subject in a manageable, practical format. It provides essential information on the management of change in organizations, with many examples from the contemporary business scene, and with numerous practical tips to make your efforts more effective.

The first chapter offers an overview of the dimensions of change used by organizations. These include structural, cultural, and process change, as well as change that aims strictly to cut costs. It also examines the different ways that these programs can be applied.

Chapter 2 explores the idea of being "change-ready," and will help you determine if your company or unit is ready for change. Effective and respected leaders and a nonhierarchical culture are shown to be key factors in change-readiness. If your organization is weak in these factors, practical advice is offered for how you can pave the way for successful change.

Chapter 3 details seven steps that will help assure the success of your change initiative. It explores the "right" and "wrong" things to do during change efforts, and offers a helpful list of "mistakes to avoid."

Implementation—the toughest part of change management—is covered in chapter 4. This chapter is organized around key implementation activities: mobilizing support, planning the initiative, encouraging behaviors that are consistent with the plan, building enabling structures, celebrating milestones, and communicating relentlessly.

Chapter 5 delves into the social and human factors involved in change. The managers and employees who populate organizational systems have identities, relationships, and emotions that are bound to be altered or destabilized by change. This accounts for some of the complexity of organizational change. As a manager you must recognize the centrality of the social systems in which change is occurring. To that end, the chapter focuses on the three sets of players encountered in every change initiative: the rank-and-file, the resisters, and the change agents.

The title of chapter 6, "Helping People Adapt," speaks for itself. Those who are forced to undergo change often go through a "mourning" process, involving a period of shock, followed by anger, and then acceptance. As a manager, understanding these stages will equip you to help your people adapt to change.

The final chapter addresses the topic of continuous change, raising questions such as: Is it possible? Can managers and employees handle it? Will too much change create more problems than it solves? This chapter will answer these questions and provide practical advice on how to sculpt your organization, via small, manageable steps, into one that is always changing and improving.

Two short appendices supplement the information provided in the rest of the book. The first of these offers a number of worksheets and checklists you can use in managing different aspects of organizational change. The second is a primer on how to hire and use consultants, who are frequently key players in change initiatives.

Although these materials will not make you an expert on change management, they do provide authoritative, *essential* advice you can use to get going and to stay on track. For those who want to learn more, a reading list is included at the back of the book.

In addition, the official Harvard Business Essentials Web site, www.elearning.hbsp.org/businesstools, offers free interactive versions of the tools introduced in this series.

The content in this book is based on a number of books, articles, and online productions of Harvard Business School Publishing, in particular: class notes prepared by Todd Jick on implementation and the problems people experience in adapting to change; the change management modules in Harvard ManageMentor®, an online service; and change management books and articles authored by Michael Beer, Bert Spector, Russell Eisenstat, Nitin Nohria, and John Kotter.

The Dimensions of Change

*Examining the Different Types
and Approaches*

Key Topics Covered in This Chapter

- *An overview of the primary types of change*

- *A discussion of two different approaches to
  change: "Theory E" (which aims to increase
  shareholder value) and "Theory O" (which
  is focused on improving organizational
  capabilities)*

- *An evaluation of which approach to change
  is best or most appropriate*

BEFORE GETTING INTO the details of managing change, it's useful to overview the types of change programs used by organizations and the different approaches to change that can be taken. This broad view will help you later as we get into the nitty-gritty of managing change.

Types of Change

Organizations typically respond to the challenges of new technologies, new competitors, new markets, and demands for greater performance with various programs, each designed to overcome obstacles and enhance business performance. Generally, these programs fall into one of the following categories:

- **Structural change.** These programs treat the organization as a set of functional parts—the "machine" model. During structural change, top management, aided by consultants, attempts to reconfigure these parts to achieve greater overall performance. Mergers, acquisitions, consolidations, and divestiture of operating units are all examples of attempts at structural change.

- **Cost cutting.** Programs such as these focus on the elimination of nonessential activities or on other methods for squeezing costs out of operations. Activities and operations that get little scrutiny during profitable years draw the attention of cost cutters when times are tough.

- **Process change.** These programs focus on altering *how* things get done. You've probably been involved with one or more of these. Examples include reengineering a loan approval process, the company's approach to handling customer warranty claims, or even how decisions are made. Process change typically aims to make processes faster, more effective, more reliable, and/or less costly.

- **Cultural change.** These programs focus on the "human" side of the organization, such as a company's general approach to doing business or the relationship between its management and employees. A shift from command-and-control management to participative management is an example of cultural change, as is any effort to reorient a company from an inwardly focused "product push" mentality to an outward-looking customer focus.

None of these change programs are easy, nor is success ever assured. A structural change—such as the acquisition of a complementary business—might appear easy, since the entire deal can be handled by a small platoon of senior managers and consultants, with input from the board of directors. But such an operation results in a need for more amorphous changes, such as eliminating redundancies and getting the acquired units to work together smoothly, which can be enormously difficult and time-consuming. And the record shows that few of these initiatives come close to meeting the expectations of their supporters. On the other hand, a change that focuses on a discrete operation, such as improving the customer service function, may be both easier to handle and more likely to succeed, since it involves a small activity set. The employees involved in that function may be able to handle the job by themselves, perhaps with a bit of coaching from a knowledgeable consultant.

If your organization is contemplating a change program, it will be helpful to determine which of the categories described above the initiative falls into, and to predict how is it likely to affect the overall company. Envisioning potential stumbling blocks in advance could prevent difficult issues from arising during the change process, and help ensure the success of the operation.

Two Different Approaches to Change

While there are many types of change programs, two very different goals typically drive a change initiative: *near-term economic improvement* or an *improvement in organizational capabilities.* Harvard Business School professors Michael Beer and Nitin Nohria coined the terms "Theory E" and "Theory O" to describe these two basic goals.[1]

Theory E: An Economic Approach

The explicit goal of Theory E change is to dramatically and rapidly increase shareholder value, as measured by improved cash flow and share price. Popular notions of employee participation and the "learning organization" take a back seat to this overarching goal. Financial crisis is usually the trigger for this approach to change. Driven to increase shareholder value, Theory E proponents rely heavily on mechanisms likely to increase short-term cash flow and share price: performance bonuses, headcount reductions, asset sales, and strategic reordering of business units. Jack Welch's 25 percent headcount reduction at GE, and his subsequent "be #1 or #2 in your market or be sold" strategy are prime examples of actions stemming from a Theory E change process.

According to Theory E, all implicit contracts between the company and its employees, such as lifetime employment, are suspended during the change effort. Individuals and units whose activities fail to demonstrate tangible value creation—for example, corporate planning or R&D—are particularly vulnerable.

The CEO and the executive team drive Theory E change from the top. Corporate departments, operating units, and employees involved in this approach are like pieces on management's strategic chessboard; they are rearranged or combined, and occasionally cashed out. Outside consultants provide advice to members of the inner circle: strategy consultants help management identify and weigh its options; valuation specialists and investment bankers arrange for asset sales and/or acquisitions; and HR consultants help with thorny layoff issues.

Theory O: An Organizational Capabilities Approach

We've all been told that the most successful and enduring organizations are those with dynamic, learning-oriented cultures and highly capable employees. Companies such as Intel, Microsoft, 3M, Schwab, and Merck come to mind. The goal of Theory O change is to develop an organizational culture that supports learning and a high-performance employee base.

Companies that follow this approach attempt to invigorate their cultures and capabilities through individual and organizational learning. And that requires high levels of employee participation, flatter organizational structure, and strong bonds between the organization and its people. Because employee commitment to change and improvement are vital for Theory O change to work, implicit contracts with employees are considered too important to break—quite the opposite from what happens in the Theory E organization. For example, when Hewlett-Packard found itself stagnating in the early 1980s, it didn't jettison people to cut costs; it reduced bureaucracy and gave people and operating units greater autonomy. That approach was consistent with HP's time-honored tradition of valuing its people assets above all others.

An organization that banks on its culture and people to drive financial success is potentially incompatible with concentrated power and direction from the top. But leaders of Theory O change are less interested in driving the success themselves than in encouraging participation within the ranks, and in fostering employee behaviors and attitudes that will sustain such change.

Which Is Best—Or Most Appropriate?

If your organization is considering a major change program, you are probably wondering which is best. Unfortunately, the record shows that neither approach is a guarantee of success. Theory E, aiming for rapid improvements in profitability, often succeeds in the short run, but does so at the expense of future vitality. By decimating employee ranks, it leaves survivors demoralized and disloyal. Any commitment they had to the company and its goals evaporates. Ironically, the people the organization hopes to retain—the brightest and most marketable employees—are among the first to snap up severance packages and look for greener pastures.

Nor do Theory E's draconian measures always produce the desired results. A survey conducted after the last wave of corporate downsizings (late 1980s through early 1990s) found that only 45 percent of downsizers reported higher operating profits.[2]

Theory O is not an ideal solution either. Reorienting corporate culture around employee commitment and learning is a noble endeavor, but it is a multiyear proposition. A successful program may produce a smarter, more adaptive employee base in four to five years, but companies that really need change cannot wait that long for results. Managers and employees, not to mention analysts and shareholders, simply aren't that patient.

Most companies studied by Beer and Nohria eschewed both pure Theory E and Theory O as solutions, preferring a mix of the two to suit their needs. Indeed, this may be the best path for your organization to follow (see "A Tale of Two Theories" for examples of the pitfalls of attempting to apply only one of the approaches).

A Tale of Two Theories

To illustrate Theory E and Theory O, Michael Beer and Nitin Nohria have described two companies in similar businesses that adopted almost pure forms of each archetype: Scott Paper used Theory E to enhance shareholder value, while Champion International used Theory O to achieve a cultural transformation aimed at increasing productivity and employee commitment. Here's how they described these initiatives to readers of the *Harvard Business Review*:

> *When Al Dunlap assumed leadership of Scott Paper in May 1994, he immediately fired 11,000 employees and sold off several*

businesses. . . . As he said in one of his speeches: "Shareholders are the number one constituency. Show me an annual report that lists six of seven constituencies, and I'll show you a mismanaged company." From a shareholder's perspective, the results of Dunlap's actions were stunning. In just 20 months, he managed to triple shareholder returns as Scott's market value rose from about $3 billion in 1994 to about $9 billion in 1995. . . . Champion's reform effort couldn't have been more different. CEO Andrew Sigler acknowledged that enhanced economic value was an appropriate target for management, but he believed that goal would be best achieved by transforming the behaviors of management, unions, and workers alike.[a]

In the end, neither company achieved its goal. Dunlap was forced to sell a demoralized and ineffective organization to Kimberly-Clark, and a languishing Champion International was sold to UPM-Kymmene. These failures contrast sharply with the successes enjoyed by companies that skillfully integrated the two approaches.

[a] Michael Beer and Nitin Nohria, "Cracking the Code of Change," *Harvard Business Review* 78, no. 3 (May–June 2000): 135.

"Companies that effectively combine hard and soft approaches to change can reap big payoffs in profitability and productivity," the authors write. "Those companies are more likely to achieve a sustainable competitive advantage [and] . . . reduce the anxiety that grips whole societies in the face of corporate restructuring."[3] They offer General Electric as an example, where former CEO Jack Welch employed both approaches in turn. First he squeezed out all of the redundancies and under-performing units through draconian Theory E methods. He then followed with change initiatives designed to improve the competitiveness of the company's culture by making it faster, less bureaucratic, and more customer-focused—a Theory O move. As described by David Ulrich:

By the late 1980s, GE was strategically strong, with thirteen major businesses, each lean, globally positioned, and number one or two in market share. Since the latter part of the 1980s, GE's management has focused on more fundamental culture change. Under the rubric Work-out, a number of initiatives involved GE employees in dismantling bureaucracies, making faster decisions, moving more quickly to serve customers, and getting rid of unnecessary work. Through town-hall meetings in which employees worked with managers to identify and eliminate unnecessary work, GE worked to incorporate the values of speed, simplicity, and self-confidence into the organization's culture.[4]

In a sense, GE's method was to fix the "hardware" first through divestitures and consolidations. Once that job was completed, it turned

TABLE 1 - 1

Key Factors in Theory E and Theory O Change

Dimensions of Change	Theory E	Theory O	Theories E and O Combined
Goals	Maximize shareholder value	Develop organizational capabilities	Embrace the paradox between economic value and organizational capability
Leadership	Manage change from the top	Encourage participation from the bottom up	Set direction from the top and engage the people below
Focus	Emphasize structure and systems	Build up corporate culture: employees' behavior and attitudes	Focus simultaneously on the hard (structures and systems) and the soft (corporate culture)
Process	Plan and establish programs	Experiment and evolve	Plan for spontaneity
Reward system	Motivate through financial incentives	Motivate through commitment—use pay as fair exchange	Use incentives to reinforce change but not to drive it
Use of consultants	Consultants analyze problems and shape solutions	Consultants support management in shaping their own solutions	Consultants are expert resources who empower employees

Source: Michael Beer and Nitin Nohria, "Cracking the Code of Change," *Harvard Business Review* 78, no. 3 (May–June 2000): 137.

its focus to the "software"—its employees and how they conducted their work.

Which approach is best for your particular situation? Only the people who are familiar with the inner workings of your company can say with any authority. To help you think through the pros and cons of each theory, table 1-1 summarizes the two archetypal change approaches—and their combination—in terms of key factors. You can tell a lot about the mind-set of your company's executives by checking off how they manage each of the six factors.

Summing Up

This chapter highlighted the different types of change initiatives observed in organizations:

- structural change

- cost cutting change

- process change

- and cultural change

It also explored two different approaches that can be taken to pursue these changes:

- Theory E change aims for a dramatic and rapid increase in shareholder value. It is driven from the top of the organization and makes heavy use of outside consultants. Theory E relies heavily on cost cutting, downsizing, and asset sales to meet its objectives.

- Theory O change aims to create higher performance by fostering a powerful culture and capable employees. It is characterized by high levels of employee participation and flatter organizational structure, and attempts to build bonds between the enterprise and its employees. Unlike Theory E, this approach to change is a long-term proposition.

2

Are You Change–Ready?

Preparing for Organizational Change

Key Topics Covered in This Chapter

- *Why leaders must be respected and effective for change to happen*

- *The role of motivation in change-readiness*

- *The importance of a nonhierarchical culture in implementing change*

- *Tips on how to become "change-ready"*

THE INFORMATION and advice given in this book will be of little use if your organization is not "change-ready." By change-ready we mean that the people and structure of the organization are prepared for and capable of change. An organization is change-ready when three conditions are present:

1. Leaders are respected and effective.

2. People feel personally motivated to change.

3. The organization is nonhierarchical and people are accustomed to collaborative work.

This chapter will delve into these conditions in greater detail and explain how you can cultivate them in your company.

Respected and Effective Leaders

Everything we know about management tells us that bad bosses—people who are neither respected nor effective—are absolute deterrents to organizational performance. They cannot retain good employees and they cannot motivate those who remain. A company can have terrific pay and benefits, employee-friendly policies, and all the other things that induce employee loyalty and retention, but a few bad apple managers can spoil the barrel. In addition, inept leaders in key positions can thwart well-designed plans to improve performance. In writing about the problem of "C performers," Beth Axelrod, Helen

Handfield-Jones, and Ed Michaels of McKinsey & Company pinpoint some of the key issues raised by "bad managers":

> [K]eeping C performers in leadership positions lowers the bar for everyone—a clear danger for any company that wants to create a performance-focused culture. C performers hire other C performers, and their continued presence discourages the people around them, makes the company a less attractive place for highly talented people, and calls into question the judgment of senior leaders.[1]

If you have lots of mediocre managers in your organization, don't expect to get very far with your change program. C performers are ineffective at motivating people to embark on difficult tasks. If it's in your capacity, culling out C performers at every level of leadership, and replacing them with individuals who are effective and respected by their people, will move you a step closer to being change-ready.

Motivation to Change

The second necessary condition for change-readiness is a high degree of motivation on the part of employees to change aspects of the organization. This motivation typically results from tangible dissatisfaction with the status quo and an eagerness for something measurably better. A certain level of nervousness, fear, or discomfort —resulting in a clear sense of *urgency*—must be in the air for real change to have a chance.

The quality revolution led by the late W. Edwards Deming demonstrated, on a broad scale, how the attitudes of individuals and institutions toward the status quo can either pave the way for change, or hold it at arm's length. Deming was a protégé of Walter Shewhart, who developed the theory and practice of statistical process control (SPC) in the 1930s at AT&T's Western Electric division. Deming diffused SPC principles to the wider world of U.S. manufacturing during the war years, but to his disappointment, those principles were abandoned and largely forgotten in the post-war era, when U.S. business found itself essentially unchallenged in the world. American manufacturing was satisfied, complacent, and comfortable, and didn't have much interest in Deming's quality principles.

Halfway around the world, however, America's competitors were extremely change-ready. Japan's industrial base had been flattened by the Allied bombings. Its resources were few, and its products were viewed as shoddy and poorly designed. Worse, millions of people were unemployed. Everyone in Japan knew that industrial revitalization was the only way out of this desperate situation. And Deming, a prophet ignored in his own land, offered a blueprint for success. As described by Richard Luecke in his book of history lessons for modern managers:

> Deming told the Japanese leaders that following [the SPC] approach would result in a "chain reaction" of good things for their companies. Improved quality would result in decreased cost (less rework, fewer delays, less scrappage), which would result in improved productivity, which would lead to the capture of markets, business survival, and more jobs.[2]

Eager and ready for change, Japan's industrial leaders embraced Deming's gospel on manufacturing quality and got workers and managers at all levels involved. Between 1950 and 1970, almost 15,000 engineers and many more thousands of factory supervisors were educated by Deming and others in the principles of statistical process control. Quality became something of an industrial religion in Japan, and Deming was its high priest.

The quality movement changed Japanese industry in fundamental ways, and those changes stuck. Before long, Japanese manufacturers managed to take over the motorcycle market, the small car market, the market for inexpensive wristwatches, and the consumer electronics market. From those beachheads, they began moving upstream in computers, high-end timepieces, and luxury automobiles. They were also taking most of the awards for excellence in design and reliability. And consumers were discovering that Japanese-made products, paradoxically, offered higher quality *and* lower cost.

Ironically, the United States—the nation that invented SPC—didn't begin to adopt quality methods in serious ways until the late 1970s, when Ford Motor Company's Donald Peterson hired Deming to teach his people SPC principles. What made Ford change-ready?

It's simple. The company was in a death spiral; it was losing money hand over fist, and the Ford name had become an acronym for "Fix Or Repair Daily." Both management and rank-and-file employees knew in their bones that something had to change. Unlike Ford, crosstown rival General Motors remained complacent, continuing to bask in the delusion that everything was just fine for another five years. In fact, when GM's own Quality & Reliability staff confronted top management with the depth of the company's quality problems, their study was dismissed. The CEO and his circle remained solid in their conviction that GM was the world's finest automaker, and the company against which all others had to be measured.[3] Only a harsh awakening would launch GM into the change it required.

Eventually, SPC principles were widely embraced by U.S. manufacturers, but not until managers and employees at many levels had lost their complacency and were ready to receive them.

Challenging Complacency

Many successful change programs grow out of crisis. Ford's "change-or-die" story was repeated at Continental Airlines, Harley-Davidson, the Martin guitar company, IBM, and many others. This raises an important question: Does an organization have to wait for a crisis before change is possible? According to Harvard Business School professor Mike Beer, the answer is no. He believes that change leaders can raise concerns about a current, problematic situation, and urge management to challenge the complacency that fosters it—without resorting to "crisis mode" tactics. He offers the following four approaches for accomplishing this goal:[4]

1. **Use information about the organization's competitive situation to generate discussion with employees about current and prospective problems.** Top management, he says, often fails to understand why employees are not concerned about productivity, customer service, or costs. Too often this is because management has failed to put employees in touch with the relevant data. In the absence of that data, everything appears to be fine.

2. **Create opportunities for employees to educate management about the dissatisfaction and problems they experience.** In some cases, top management is out of touch with weaknesses of the business or emerging threats—things that frontline employees understand through daily experience on the factory floor or in face-to-face dealings with customers. If this is your company's problem, find ways to improve communications between top management and frontline people.

3. **Create dialogue on the data.** Providing data is one thing. Creating dialogue on the data is something entirely different and more productive. Dialogue should aim for a joint understanding of company problems. Dialogue is a means by which both managers and employees can inform each other of their assumptions and their diagnoses.

4. **Set high standards and expect people to meet them.** The act of setting high standards creates dissatisfaction with the current level of performance.

Complacency is a barrier to change. When people are comfortable with the way things are, they are oblivious to things that need changing. How complacent is your organization? Table 2-1 details some signs of complacency to be on the lookout for. Challenge every one you see!

Rewards

In exploring the subject of motivating change, it is important to include some discussion of rewards. Almost all fundamental changes in organizations involve some changes in the rewards system. Most people would agree that personal rewards act as a powerful "invisible hand" in altering behavior and encouraging change.

Much academic research has reached what seems to be an obvious conclusion: a well-aligned compensation system encourages more of the behaviors (or outcomes) you want and fewer of the behaviors (or outcomes) you hope to discourage. If you want a clear example, you needn't look any farther than Nucor's steelmaking

TABLE 2 - 1

Is Your Organization Complacent?

Signs of Complacency	Examples
No highly visible crisis.	The company is not losing money; no big layoffs are threatened.
The company measures itself against low standards.	The company compares itself to the industry average, not to the industry leader.
Organizational structure focuses attention on narrow functional goals instead of broad business performance.	Marketing has one measurement criterion; manufacturing has another that is unrelated. Only the CEO uses broader measures (return on invested capital, economic value added, etc.).
Planning and control systems are rigged to make it easy for everyone to make their functional goals.	The typical manager or employee can work for months without encountering an unsatisfied or frustrated customer or supplier.
Performance feedback is strictly internal. Feedback from customers, suppliers, and shareholders is not encouraged.	The culture dictates that external feedback is either without value or likely to be uninformed. "Customers really don't know what they want. We do."
Evidence that change is needed results in finger-pointing.	"It's manufacturing's problem, not ours."
Management focuses on marginal issues.	"The ship is sinking. Let's rearrange the deck chairs."
The culture sends subliminal messages of success.	Plush offices, wood paneling, and fine art adorn corporate offices.
Management believes its own press releases and mythology.	"We are the greatest ad agency in the country. We set the standard for our industry."

Source: Adapted from John P. Kotter, *Leading Change* (Boston, MA: Harvard Business School Press, 1996), 39–41.

operations, where output and pay are closely linked, and where employees are more productive than steelworkers anywhere else.

Less obvious to the change planner/leader is which behaviors and outputs to reward. These must be situationally determined. Making a mistake in the rewards regime can throw a monkey wrench into the works. So, to make your organization more change-ready, check the alignment of your rewards system and the behaviors you want to encourage. Business professor Edward Lawler makes the point that different reward systems are more appropriate at different phases of a change initiative.[5] For example:

- Performance-based pay plans, such as stock options and profit sharing, are most appropriate during the motivation stage of change.

- During the implementation phase, bonuses for achieving performance targets and successful implementation are useful.

- Finally, once change has been effected, the organization may want to change to a pay-for-performance regime that focuses on the strategic performance and the attraction/retention of talented people.

Rewards alone cannot produce desired changes if the people charged with making change happen lack the knowledge, information, and power they need to do the job. Thus, rewards must be part of a larger package of transformational levers.

A Nonhierarchical Organization

If an organization needs to undergo economically driven change, involving selling off assets, laying people off, and reorganizing around a more manageable core, a hierarchical structure may not be an impediment. In fact, a highly managed, command-and-control structure may be optimal for such an initiative to take hold. But other types of change—of processes and culture—require something much different.

For such changes, hierarchy must be reduced before an organization is truly change-ready. Trying to change a hierarchical, command-and-control organization is like swimming upstream. It can be done, but it will wear you out and reduce your odds of success. Here's why:

- In hierarchical organizations, decisions are made at the top and passed down through intermediaries. But people resist solutions imposed by people who lack familiarity with day-to-day operations.

- Organizations that aim to change need a certain number of entrepreneurial employees—people who like to try new things and who are comfortable with taking risks. But these entrepreneurial spirits are usually rarities in hierarchical firms.

- Hierarchy protects two enemies of change: bureaucracy (the protectors of "how we do things around here") and a sense of entitlement among employees—that is, a sense that "If I just stay in my little cubicle and continue doing what I've always done, my job will be guaranteed."

- Effective change demands collaboration between willing and motivated parties. Unfortunately, hierarchical companies are better at telling people what to do than at getting employees to collaborate.

The problem with hierarchy is that it simply doesn't facilitate collaborative work—one of the important skills that employees must have in a change-ready organization. When hierarchy dominates the culture, corporate commissars do all the thinking, control access to information, and tell everyone what to do. Under these circumstances, collaboration is an unnatural act.

There are two ways to overcome the problem of hierarchy. The first is to push the organization toward a more decentralized business model in which individual units have greater autonomy. This in itself would be a major "Theory O" change initiative. If that organizational makeover is not possible in the short run, then follow the second course: create opportunities for collaboration between people in different units and at different levels. For example, set up cross-functional teams to deal with key issues such as employee benefits or improvement of processes that span several departments.

Becoming Change-Ready

If your organization isn't change-ready, the following sections outline things you can do to push it closer to this goal.

Do a Unit–by–Unit Change–Readiness Assessment

Although the organization as a whole may be unprepared, specific units are often ready to go—that is, they have respected and effective leaders, they are motivated to change, and people in those units are accustomed to working together in collaborative ways. Start change programs in these prepared units, and use them as test beds for your change initiative.

**Develop More Participative Approaches to
How Everyday Business Is Handled**

Do what you can to develop the "habits" of participative work. Specifically:

- push decision-making down to the lowest possible levels;

- begin sharing information freely;

- make communication a two-way street—talk, but also listen;

- eliminate unnecessary symbols of hierarchy and unequal status— executive lunch rooms and parking spaces, high- and low-status offices;

- encourage participatory management;

- get into the trenches with frontline employees—and encourage other managers to do the same;

- give people practice in collaborative work between functions by attacking projects and problems through cross-functional teams; and

- help people see the "why" of change, and work with them to discover the "what."

Give People a Voice

Voice empowers people to act. Richard Axelrod writes that:

The cornerstone of any democratic process is voice—*the power to be heard and to influence outcomes. Maximizing voice means widening the circle of involvement to encompass those likely to be affected by the change process, including those who might be opposed or who think differently. When people really believe their voice counts, a critical mass for change spontaneously emerges. But in companies that lack interactive discourse, it's harder to mobilize the energy and the innovation required to reverse sagging fortunes.*[6]

John Kotter makes the point that employees generally won't help—or cannot help—with a change effort if they feel relatively powerless or voiceless. He has also identified barriers to empowerment that the rest of us are likely to overlook (see figure 2-1). The formal structure of an organization is one of these barriers. If, for example, the goal or vision is to "focus on the customer," an organizational structure that fragments resources and responsibilities into disconnected silos will be an impediment to change. Likewise, a structure built on phalanxes of middle managers will probably block any plan to empower lower-level employees.

FIGURE 2-1

Barriers to Empowerment

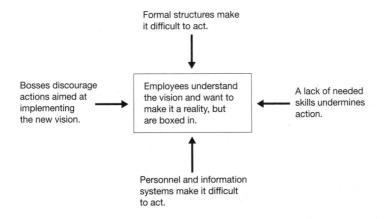

Source: John P. Kotter, *Leading Change* (Boston, MA: Harvard Business School Press, 1996), 102.

If you're serious about making the organization change-ready, you'll have to eliminate or lower these barriers. (See "Tips for Empowering People" for more information about this process.)

Drive Out Fear

The quality methodology developed by W. Edwards Deming included fourteen points for effective management. One of those points urged managers to drive fear out of the workplace. An organizational culture dominated by fear is incapable of serious change. Fear encourages everyone to avoid risks, hunker down, and keep their mouths shut—even to conceal disappointing results. Consider this example, which demonstrates how an atmosphere of fear hides the truth and keeps people from coming to grips with needed change.

Tips for Empowering People

Employees who are empowered are essential for successful organizational change. Here are some tips to empower the people who work for you:

- Encourage innovative thinking.

- Demonstrate respect for employees—and do it regularly.

- Delegate, and don't micromanage.

- Extend trust. If you are dissatisfied with the result, identify the cause and work on it.

- Be flexible, and demonstrate that flexibility to others.

- Release control of a project to others at the first opportunity.

- Encourage risk-taking and be tolerant of failures.

- Spread decision-making authority around.

Back in the early 1980s, before General Motors's leadership faced up to its quality problems, a group of managers and engineers conducted a study to determine what had gone wrong with the company's X-car and J-car projects, which were plagued with quality problems in their early production years. As described by Gregory Watson in his book *Strategic Benchmarking:*

> *J-car veterans purged themselves in these [interview] sessions, describing how the pressure to keep to schedule and avoid reporting bad news to top management had led them to take shortcuts, compromise on quality, and even fudge test results on the J-car. It was revealed that when then-President and CEO James McDonald arrived with his entourage at the Arizona test track to try out the pre-production J-car, he unknowingly got behind the wheel of a vehicle whose engine had been secretly souped up and filled with special fuel to conceal its anemic performance. The test track itself had been redesigned during the previous few days to eliminate grades the car could not master.[7]*

Obviously, change cannot happen in an environment gripped with fear. For example, people in despotic nations know that the best way to survive is to shut up, follow orders, and cover up mistakes when necessary. But before long, these countries find themselves outpaced by their more open rivals. Companies are no different. Employees at all levels must feel free to challenge the status quo, identify problems, and suggest solutions—even when their views conflict with those of the leadership. They must also feel free to try new things without fear of retribution if they fail.

Summing Up

Launching a change initiative is not likely to succeed if the organization is not change-ready. This chapter described three characteristics of change-readiness that your company should possess before you launch a change initiative:

- **The organization has effective and respected leaders.** Leaders who lack those qualities cannot get people to change. If you don't have the right kinds of leaders, get them.

- **People in the organization are personally motivated to change.** They are sufficiently dissatisfied with the status quo that they are willing to make the effort and accept the risks involved with doing something new. Even in the absence of a crisis, good managers can get people motivated to change.

- **The organization has a nonhierarchical structure.** Hierarchy may present no impediment to a strictly economically driven change program, but it is a barrier to all others. Managers need to either reduce the hierarchy or work around it by giving people collaborative work assignments.

In addition, four suggestions were offered for making an organization change-ready:

- Do a unit-by-unit change-readiness assessment.

- Develop more participative approaches to how everyday business is handled.

- Give people a voice.

- Drive out fear.

3

Seven Steps to Change

A Systematic Approach

Key Topics Covered in This Chapter

- *A description of a seven-step change process*

- *An explanation of the roles that leaders, managers, and HR play during this process*

- *Tips on mistakes to avoid during implementation*

I F Y O U ' V E B E E N around big corporations for any length of time, you have probably been on the receiving end of several change programs. Here's a typical scenario:

All employees are assembled in the cafeteria where the CEO, flanked by the head of human resources and a consultant in a thousand-dollar suit, delivers a speech on yet another plan to make your company more productive and profitable. In years past, plans for quality circles, service excellence, a pay-for-performance system, and process reengineering were tried. Today it's The New Thing. The consultant then touts the virtues of this panacea, points to a handful of companies that have used it to revitalize their performance, and describes what it can do here. Eventually pizza is served and everyone goes back to work, muttering "Here we go again."

If this little scenario sounds less than promising, let's speculate on some reasons why. If you had been in that audience, you'd probably be thinking:

"Why is this important?"

"What's in it for me?"

"How do these people know what the problems are? They haven't even bothered to ask *us*."

"Do they really think they can change the entire company at once?"

"How much of our time and their money will they sink into this dry hole?"

If this scenario seems overly contrived and pessimistic, consider this: In aggregate, the scorecard for change programs is very disappointing. By some estimates, 70 percent of change initiatives fail to meet their objectives.[1] As author John Kotter once put it, "If you were to grade them using the old fashioned A, B, C, D, and F, I'd be surprised if an impartial jury would give 10% of these efforts an A. But I'm not saying that 90% deserve a D either. What is tragic is that there are so many C-pluses. It's one thing to get a C-plus on a paper; it's another when millions of dollars or thousands of jobs are at stake."[2]

Clearly, organizations need to do better. And they can if they approach change with the right attitude, from the right angle, and with a solid set of action *steps*—which is what this chapter will offer.

The Seven Steps

Back in 1990, Michael Beer and his colleagues Russell Eisenstat and Bert Spector identified a number of steps that general managers at business unit and plant levels could use to create real change. Those steps produced a self-reinforcing circle of commitment, coordination, and employee competency—all bedrocks of effective change.[3] Their steps have lost none of their potency over the years since their work was published, and so we will cover several of them here in detail. In addition, we add two others: one borrowed from General Electric's Management Development Center (step 3), and another suggested by Robert Schaffer and Harvey Thomson (step 4).

You can use these steps to guide your own change efforts.

Step 1. Mobilize Energy and Commitment through Joint Identification of Business Problems and Their Solutions

The starting point of any effective change effort, according to Beer et al., is a clear definition of the business problem. Problem identification answers the most important question that affected personnel want to know: Why must we do this? The answer to this question can lay the foundation for motivation, and thus must be answered convincingly. The "why" of change may be a looming crisis, years of declining profit margins, or research that indicates that the public doesn't like doing business with your company.

Answering "why" is essential not just for its motivating potential, but also because it creates a sense of urgency, and, as we've discussed, change won't happen without urgency. People will not grapple with the pain and effort of serious change without a sense that "We have to do this—like it or not!"

How much urgency is required? Here's a good rule of thumb: Your change goals cannot be achieved unless 75 percent of managers are genuinely convinced that sticking with the status quo is more dangerous or more painful than striking out on another path.[4]

Though problem identification is a must, *how* the problem is identified is also important. Motivation and commitment to change are greatest when the people who will have to make the change and live with it are instrumental in *identifying the problem and planning its solution*. This is nothing more than common sense. Being involved in pinpointing the issue also assures the rank and file that the identified problem is the right one.

The idea that the people closest to a situation can identify the problem is something that senior executives and staff people sometimes fail to appreciate. People at the top often assume (wrongly) that they have identified the entire problem. The truth is that they generally understand *part* of the problem but fail to understand it *in toto*. Their top-down approach results in two serious errors: The problem is improperly defined, and the solution is too narrowly drawn. Either error can torpedo the change program. The same can happen when the CEO puts a consultant on the case. Consulting companies have a habit of creating solutions to problems and then peddling them like bottled medicine to organizations that appear to have the right symptoms. Unfortunately, unlike medicinal treatments, off-the-shelf business improvement solutions created by consultants are not subjected to rigorous testing. No objective testing by disinterested parties is done to determine their efficacy or the conditions under which they work or fail. There are no control groups, and no control of the many variables that affect success and failure. And there is no warning of possible "side effects." Nor does effectiveness in one operating unit assure effectiveness in others within the same company. So beware of cookie-cutter solutions.

Top-driven change also creates people problems. People resist having solutions imposed on them by individuals who lack intimate familiarity with their day-to-day operations. Their resistance is expressed through a lack of motivation and commitment to change. This is not to say that top management has no role to play in organizational change. It is generally their job to sound the warning that substantive change is needed, and their support for a change initiative is essential. As John Kotter has written: "[M]ajor change is impossible unless the head of the organization is an active supporter."[5] In his experience, successful transformation is supported by a coalition of key individuals that include the CEO, division general manager, and other leaders including, in some instances, a key customer or union official. But there is a big difference between top-level support and top-level control.

The second part of this step, after defining the business problem, is developing a solution to the problem. Here again employees should be involved. A good example of this was seen in the case of Philips, the Dutch electronics giant. In the early 1990s, newly appointed CEO Jan Timmer initiated a change program aimed at restoring the company's growth and profitability. He mobilized energy and commitment by generating a sense of urgency and by getting everyone involved. Though it began with the top one hundred executives, the Philips initiative cascaded to each succeeding level. As described in an article by Paul Strebel:

> *Timmer knew that he could not accomplish his goals unless managers and subordinates throughout the company were also committed to change. Employees' concerns about this corporate initiative had to be addressed. . . . At workshops and training programs, employees at all levels talked about the consequences and objectives of change. Timmer reached out via company "town meetings" to answer questions and talk about the future. His approach made people feel included, and his direct style encouraged them to support him. It soon became clear that employees were listening and the company was changing.[6]*

You can do something similar in your company or your unit. The first task is to bring people face-to-face with urgent business problems and their root causes. Then make sure they understand the possible consequences—in personal terms—if those problems are not solved: bonuses eliminated, layoffs, possible sale of the company, and so forth. Doing so will puncture any sense of complacency.

If waning profitability is the problem, hold a meeting in which the decline in profits is demonstrated graphically. Then involve people from different levels in ferreting out the causes of profit decline. Is lower revenue the problem, higher costs, or both? Ask them to dig farther and find the root causes. If higher costs are the cause of profit decline, which specific costs are on the rise—and why? How could those rising costs be reversed? (For more on identifying the business problem, see "Motivate by Finding Gaps.")

Step 2. Develop a Shared Vision of How to Organize and Manage for Competitiveness

The people in charge of change must develop a clear vision of an altered and improved future. They must also be able to communicate that vision to others in ways that make the benefits of change clear. In communicating the vision, be very specific about how the change will: 1) improve the business (through greater customer satisfaction, product quality, sales revenues, or productivity), and 2) how those improvements will benefit employees. Employee benefits might include higher pay, larger bonuses, new opportunities for advancement, or greater job security.

Price Pritchett, a change management expert at Dallas-based Pritchett & Associates, says that 20 percent of employees tend to support a change from the start, another 50 percent are fence-sitters, and the remaining 30 percent tend to oppose the change. Those fence-sitters and resisters must be converted and enlisted to participate in realizing the vision. It isn't enough to just identify the problem and agree on how to proceed. You have to get people excited and involved.

An effective vision can get most employees on the side of change. But what constitutes an effective vision? John Kotter has suggested six characteristics. From his perspective, an effective vision must:[7]

Motivate by Finding Gaps

Effecting meaningful change requires a clear understanding of current conditions and desired outcomes. By determining what is critical to the success of the organization in each of its core processes—for example, marketing, manufacturing, satisfying clients—and by detailing the desired future states, you and your team have an opportunity to identify any "gaps" in organizational performance. These gaps can be the basis for broad-based motivation to change.

Xerox Discovers a Critical Cost Gap

In 1979, Xerox's copier division set out to benchmark its productivity measures against those of rising foreign competitors. Xerox had invented the copier industry, and virtually owned it until this time. But now Japanese companies were coming out with smaller, less expensive, and more reliable models. Xerox was aware of a substantial cost difference between their operations and those of these new competitors, but lacked the details.

Working through its Japanese partner, Fuji Xerox, the American company performed *gap analysis* to identify and measure what turned out to be a shocking cost gap. Its Japanese rivals were profitably selling their machines in the United States at less than Xerox's own cost of production! This was startling news. Once the gap was quantified, it became the centerpiece of a change initiative that introduced the quality and benchmarking techniques that successfully reformed Xerox.

1. describe a desirable future—one that people would be happy to have right now if they could;

2. be compelling—that is, it must be so much better than the current state that they will gladly undertake the effort and sacrifice as necessary to attain it;

3. be realistic—the vision must be perceived as being within the grasp of a hardworking group of people;

4. be focused—for example, it should limit itself to a manageable and coherent set of goals, such as six sigma quality, or customer service that resolves a customer's problem with a single phone call;

5. be flexible—that is, able to adapt to changing circumstances; and

6. be easy to communicate to different levels.

Two cautions about the "vision." First, a powerful vision can inspire and motivate. But a vision must be "translatable" by managers and employees into actions that will produce tangible results. So always ask: "What *specifically* should this vision produce?" It might be a 25 percent reduction in production rejects, a 20 percent profit improvement next year, or a loan approval decision in one day instead of three. Whatever it is for your organization, don't allow a lofty vision to crowd out specific improvement goals.

The second caution is to make the vision compatible with the core values of the organization—the values that have sustained it over the years. If a vision does not resonate with those values, the change process could invite conflicted behavior and confusion about what's the right thing to do.

Step 3. Identify the Leadership

Be sure that you have a visible leader and sponsor of change, someone who owns and leads the change initiative. The leadership must act as champion, assemble the resources needed for the project, and take responsibility for success or failure. This is a step that General Electric insists on for its own change initiatives. What kinds of people are most suitable for change leadership? Successful change leaders, according to Beer, Eisenstat, and Spector, share three characteristics:[8]

1. They have a persistent belief that revitalization is key to competitiveness and a deep conviction that fundamental change will have a major impact on the bottom line—and they aren't shy about it.

2. They articulate their conviction in the form of a credible and compelling vision. People won't buy into the pain and effort of change unless they can see a future state that is tangibly better—and better for them—than the one they have at the moment. Successful change leaders can form such a vision and communicate it in compelling terms.

3. They have the people-skills and organizational know-how to implement their vision. This ability to get the job done, per Beer et al., is a function of operating experience. "Only those leaders with a depth of operating management experience seemed able to successfully implement their vision of a revitalized organization."[9] A lack of operating knowledge, according to their studies, fatally undermines an individual's ability to make change happen.

This last point contains a clear warning: As you identify leadership for change, don't be tempted to put the human resources department in charge. HR may be respected for its know-how in areas of personnel and benefits, but it is often seen as clueless about operations. The same goes for other staff functionaries. Again, control and responsibility must be situated in the units undergoing change, and handled by the unit leaders.

Step 4. Focus on Results, Not on Activities

Many companies make the mistake of focusing measurement and managerial attention on training, team-creation, and other activities that—logically—should produce desirable results down the road. Per Robert Schaffer and Harvey Thomson's research, these activities "sound good, look good, and allow mangers to feel good," but contribute little or nothing to bottom-line performance.[10] They cite the example of one major enterprise that, after three years, proudly pointed to forty-eight improvement teams, high morale, and two completed quality improvement plans—but absolutely *no* measurable performance improvements!

As an antidote to activity-focused programs, Schaffer and Thomson recommend a shift to measurable short-term performance improvement goals, even though the change campaign is a long-term, sustained one. For example, "Within ninety days we will reduce fuel costs by 15 percent." Results-driven improvement efforts bypass lengthy periods of preparation, training course development, and other "rituals" of change. (See "Putting Results-Driven Change into Practice" for an expanded example of results-driven change.)

Putting Results-Driven Change into Practice

Step 4 advocates a focus on results instead of a focus on activities. Here is an example of how one organization used that advice.

The Eddystone Generating Station of Philadelphia Electric, once the world's most efficient fossil-fuel plant, illustrates the successful shift from activity-centered to results-driven improvement. As Eddystone approached its thirtieth anniversary, its thermal efficiency—the amount of electricity produced from each ton of coal burned—had declined significantly. The problem was serious enough that top management was beginning to question the plant's continued operation.

The station's engineers had initiated many corrective actions, including installing a state-of-the-art computerized system to monitor furnace efficiency, upgrading plant equipment and materials, and developing written procedures for helping operating staff run the plant more efficiently. But because the innovations were not built into the day-to-day operating routine of the plant, thermal efficiency deteriorated whenever the engineers turned their attention elsewhere.

In September 1990, the superintendent of operations decided to take a results-driven approach to improve thermal efficiency. He and his management team committed to achieve a specific incremental improvement of thermal efficiency worth about $500,000 annually—*without* any additional plant investment. To get started, they identified a few improvements that they could accomplish within three months and established teams to tackle each one.

A five-person team of operators and maintenance employees and one supervisor took responsibility for reducing steam loss from hundreds of steam valves throughout the plant. The team members started by eliminating all the leaks in one area of the plant. Then they moved on to other areas. In the process, they invented improvements in valve-packing practices and devised new methods for reporting leaks. Another employee team was assigned the task of reducing heat that escaped through openings in the huge furnaces. For its first subproject, the group ensured that all ninety-six inspection doors on the furnace walls were operable and were closed when not in use. Still another team, this one committed to reducing the amount of unburned carbon that passed through the furnace, began by improving the operating effectiveness of the station's coal-pulverizer mills in order to improve the carbon burn rate.

Management charged each of these cross-functional teams not merely with studying and recommending but also with producing measurable results in a methodical, step-by-step fashion. A steering committee of station managers met every two weeks to review progress and help overcome obstacles. A variety of communication mechanisms built awareness of the project and its progress. For example, to launch the process, the steering committee piled two tons of coal in the station manager's parking space to dramatize the hourly cost of poor thermal efficiency. In a series of "town meetings" with all employees, managers explained the reason for the effort and how it would work. Newsletters reviewed progress on the projects—including the savings realized—and credited employees who had contributed to the effort.

As each team reached its goal, the steering committee, in consultation with supervisors and employees, identified the next series of performance improvement goals, such as the reduction

Continued

of the plant's own energy consumption, and commissioned a number of teams and individuals to implement a new round of projects. By the end of the first year, efficiency improvements were saving the company over $1 million a year, double the original goal.

Beyond the monetary gains—gains achieved with negligible investment—Eddystone's organizational structure began to change in profound ways. What had been a hierarchical, tradition-bound organization became more flexible and open to change. Setting and achieving ambitious short-term goals became part of the plant's regular routine as managers pushed decisions further and further down into the organization. Eventually, the station manager disbanded the steering committee, and now everyone who manages improvement projects reports directly to the senior management team. Eddystone managers and workers at all levels have invented a number of highly creative efficiency-improving processes. A change so profound could never have happened by sending all employees to team training classes and then telling them, "Now you are empowered; go to it."

In the course of accomplishing its results, Eddystone management introduced many of the techniques that promoters of activity-centered programs insist must be drilled into the organization for months or years before gains can be expected: employees received training in various analytical techniques; team-building exercises helped teams achieve their goals more quickly; teams introduced new performance measurements as they were needed; and managers analyzed and redesigned work processes. But unlike activity-centered programs, the results-driven work teams introduced innovations only if they could contribute to the realization of short-term goals. They did not inject innovations wholesale in the hope that they would somehow generate better results. There was never any doubt that responsibility for results was in the hands of accountable managers.

SOURCE: Robert H. Schaffer and Harvey A. Thomson, "Successful Change Programs Begin with Results," *Harvard Business Review* 70, no. 1 (January–February 1992): 87–88.

Step 5. Start Change at the Periphery, Then Let It Spread to Other Units without Pushing It from the Top

The likelihood of success is greatest when change is instigated in small, fairly autonomous units. Changing an entire organization at once is much more difficult and less likely to succeed. Once change on a smaller scale is accomplished and witnessed by employees in adjacent units, diffusion of the change initiative throughout the organization is much more likely.

SQA, an innovative unit of Herman Miller Company, a leading office furniture manufacturer, provides a powerful example of diffusion based on success in one unit. SQA, which stands for "simple, quick, affordable," was a fairly autonomous unit designed to serve the small businesses furniture market. Senior management gave this unit the freedom it needed to develop a new, faster, and low-cost approach to manufacturing and fulfillment. Personnel in that unit totally redesigned their furniture building process—from order-taking to delivery—basing it on digital connectivity, mass customization, and a new relationship with supply-chain partners. By the time the makeover was complete, SQA had cut the order-to-shipment cycle from eight weeks to less than one week. On-time shipments, a rarity in the industry, reached 99.6 percent. Better yet, revenue growth for SQA was outpacing the rest of Herman Miller, and its profit margins eclipsed not only those of the larger organization, but the furniture industry as a whole.[11]

Naturally, the parent company sought to emulate SQA's methods. To help things along, Herman Miller's top management promoted and "repotted" SQA managers and operations personnel into responsible positions elsewhere in the organization. From those positions, former SQA people were able to teach others about their fast, mass-customized, and on-time approach to manufacturing. They were positioned to motivate and guide change more broadly within the corporation.

Everett Rogers's work on the diffusion of innovation provides a useful guide to our expectations for the spread of change from one unit of an organization to another.[12] Per Rogers, we can expect a greater probability of success if the change contemplated has the following features:

- clear advantages over the status quo;

- compatibility with peoples' deeply-held values, experiences, and needs;

- requirements that are understandable;

- the option for people to experiment with the change model on a small scale; and

- the possibility for people to observe the result of the change in another setting.

Each of these characteristics, not surprisingly, applied to the SQA case.

Step 6. Institutionalize Success through Formal Policies, Systems, and Structures

Getting an organization to change requires risk-taking and effort by many people. So once the objective is achieved, the last thing you want is for all your hard-earned gains to slip away. And they will if you don't take steps to prevent it. Gains can be consolidated and cemented through policies that describe how work is to be done, through information systems, and through new reporting relationships. For example, once it had achieved a key goal—over 99 percent on-time deliveries of furniture orders—SQA institutionalized its gains through a performance measurement system that kept everyone's focus on that metric. Everyone in the production facility, from the top to bottom, was expected to know the current level of on-time delivery, and various rewards were tied to it.

To follow through on the change process, it is critical that employees be as concerned with institutionalizing the "journey" as with implementing the process itself. *Continuous* improvement is the ultimate goal.

Step 7. Monitor and Adjust Strategies in Response to Problems in the Change Process

Change programs almost never proceed according to plan. All types of unanticipated problems crop up as people move forward. Developments in the external environment can also affect what's going on inside the company. So change leaders must be flexible and adaptive, and their plans must be sufficiently robust to accommodate alterations in schedules, sequencing, and personnel.

To assess your organization's approach to change based on the seven steps outlined in this section, use table 3-1, "Self-Diagnosis."

TABLE 3 - 1

Self-Diagnosis

Now that you are acquainted with the seven steps of successful change, do a little diagnosis of your own organization. Consider how it has approached change in the past and how it is approaching any current initiatives. Then score it using this brief diagnostic test, using a 1–5 scale (1=strongly disagree, 5=strongly agree).

Our organization . . .	Score
Mobilizes energy and commitment to change through joint diagnosis of business problems	_____
Develops a shared vision of how to organize and manage for competitiveness	_____
Identifies leadership	_____
Focuses on results, not on activities	_____
Spreads change to other units without pushing it from the top	_____
Institutionalizes success through formal policies, systems, and structures	_____
Monitors and adjusts strategies in response to problems in the change process	_____

How does your organization fare on these parameters? A score of three or less in any category points to serious weaknesses that you'll want to identify and correct.

Roles for Leaders, Managers, and HR

By definition, leaders create an appealing vision of the future and then develop a logical strategy for making it a reality. They also motivate people to pursue the vision, even in the face of obstacles. Managers, on the other hand, have the job of making complex tasks run smoothly. They have to work out the implementation details, round up the required resources, and keep employee energy channeled in the right direction. While leaders create a vision and plan for extending the train tracks into new territory, managers get the tracks built and make sure that the trains run on time. Thus, it is clear why the seven steps of change outlined here require effective leaders *and* managers, at all levels of the organization.

The distinction between leaders and managers, of course, is fuzzy and often arbitrary in practice. An effective leader always needs managerial skills, and every competent manager provides leadership to his or her direct reports. To evaluate your own effectiveness as a leader, it might be helpful to take the self-diagnostic test found in appendix A.

John Kotter has described the relationship of leadership and management in a simple two-by-two matrix, shown in figure 3-1. Here we see that transformation goes nowhere when both leadership and management are found wanting. Good short-term results are feasible when *either* effective leadership *or* effective managers are involved. But to enjoy long-term transformation success, both must be present.

HR professionals also have an important role to play in the success of change initiatives. We stated earlier that putting human resource personnel in charge of a change program simply paves the way to failure. Line operators—and not staff people from HR or other support functions—must lead the way within their own units. HR people, however, can play a critical supportive role by:

- helping management with the hiring and assignment of consultants;

- reassigning and/or outplacing personnel displaced by change;

FIGURE 3 - 1

The Relationship of Leadership and Management

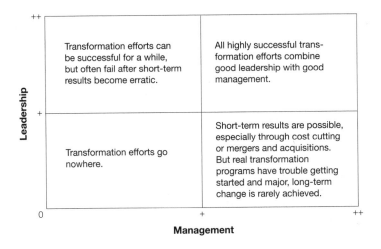

Leadership / Management quadrant:

- (High Leadership, Low Management): Transformation efforts can be successful for a while, but often fail after short-term results become erratic.
- (High Leadership, High Management): All highly successful transformation efforts combine good leadership with good management.
- (Low Leadership, Low Management): Transformation efforts go nowhere.
- (Low Leadership, High Management): Short-term results are possible, especially through cost cutting or mergers and acquisitions. But real transformation programs have trouble getting started and major, long-term change is rarely achieved.

Source: John P. Kotter, *Leading Change* (Boston, MA: Harvard Business School Press, 1996), 129.

- arranging for employee training;

- facilitating meetings and off-site conferences; and

- helping institutionalize successful change through employee development, rewards, and organizational design.

Leaders, managers, and HR must all understand their unique role in a change process and play together as part of a team. In addition, each must recognize the critical role of rank and file employees, who must be active throughout the change effort.

Mistakes to Avoid

It is possible to get halfway to success in your change initiative by simply avoiding common mistakes:

- **Don't try to impose a canned solution developed somewhere else.** Instead, develop the solution within the unit that needs change.

- **Don't place your bets on a companywide solution driven from the top.** There are some instances where this has worked, but usually only in cases where the company was heading down the tubes—and everyone knew it. If the company is large, the odds of changing an entire business in a single masterstroke are slim. Make the solution specific to the unit or units that need change.

- **Don't put HR in charge.** Put responsibility on the shoulders of unit leaders, and let them run their own show—with top management support.

- **Don't bank on a technical fix alone.** Businesses are social systems, not machines. To be effective, a technical fix must fit comfortably within the social fabric of the workplace, otherwise the workplace's immune system will attack it. Technical solutions usually miss the root causes of problems and fail to deal with the attitudes, skills, and motivations associated with them. In one classic case, a mining company's engineering solution to production efficiency was technically superior, but inadvertently broke up employee groups that had learned to work together and to support each other in a dangerous environment. The miners resisted the technical solution because it failed to account for how they worked together.

- **Don't attempt to change everything at once.** The biggest error of top-driven programmatic change is that it tries to do too much at once. Unless the entire organization is in crisis, begin change at the periphery, in units far from corporate headquarters, where local managers and their people can run the show and maintain control. That's what happened at Herman Miller, where the substantive change initially took place in its small operating unit, SQA. It's unlikely that the same success would have been achieved had Herman Miller tried to change everything in every one of its operating units in a bold stroke.

Summing Up

This chapter presented seven steps for creating change. They are:

- **Step 1. Mobilize energy and commitment through joint identification of business problems and their solutions.** Remember: You can't order energy and commitment the way you would a monthly report; but you can generate energy and commitment if you involve people in the process.

- **Step 2. Develop a shared vision of how to organize and manage for competitiveness.** The last thing you want are several competing visions of what should be done. And once you have the vision, be sure that people see it as in their personal best interest.

- **Step 3. Identify the leadership.** You need the best people involved, and you need them at all levels. Look to the managers of change-targeted units for that leadership. *Do not* put leadership in the hands of staff personnel.

- **Step 4. Focus on results, not on activities.** Don't get wrapped up in "sound good, look good, feel good" activities. Concentrate on things that will contribute directly and tangibly to bottom-line improvement.

- **Step 5. Start change at the periphery, then let it spread to other units without pushing it from the top.** You are much more likely to change the entire organization by encouraging change in peripheral units, and letting that change spread.

- **Step 6. Institutionalize success through formal policies, systems, and structures.** And don't forget to implement ways to measure the change!

- **Step 7. Monitor and adjust strategies in response to problems in the change process.** Remember that some people will quit, some elements of your change agenda will fail, and competitors may change their tactics. So be flexible.

Also covered in this chapter was a list of typical mistakes to avoid:

- imposing a canned solution;

- driving change from the top;

- putting HR in charge;

- banking on a technical solution; and

- trying to change everything at once.

   If you implement each of the seven steps effectively, and are able to avoid the common mistakes, your change goals are likely to be met.

Implementation

Putting Your Plan in Motion

Key Topics Covered in This Chapter

- *How to enlist the support and involvement of key people in a change initiative*

- *Tips for crafting a good implementation plan*

- *The importance of supporting the plan with consistent behaviors*

- *How to develop enabling structures (i.e., training, pilot programs, and a reward system)*

- *Ways to celebrate milestones*

- *The importance of relentless communication*

- *The role of consultants*

ONCE people are convinced that change is necessary, and that the change vision is the right one, it's time to move forward with implementation.

Implementation rarely proceeds smoothly. Once people get into the nitty-gritty of implementing their change initiative, they discover that there is no tidy, step-by-step march to the envisioned future. Mistakes are made. External factors upset schedules. Key people quit or are transferred. Different groups forget to communicate with each other.

A survey conducted in the mid-1980s identified seven implementation problems that occurred in at least 60 percent of the ninety-three firms polled:[1]

1. Implementation took more time than originally allocated (76 percent).

2. Major problems surfaced during implementation that had not been identified beforehand (74 percent).

3. Coordination of implementation activities (for example, task forces or committees) was not effective enough (66 percent).

4. Competing activities and crises distracted attention from implementing this strategic decision (64 percent).

5. Capabilities (skill and abilities) of employees involved with the implementation were not sufficient (63 percent).

6. Training and instruction given to lower-level employees were not adequate (62 percent).

7. Uncontrollable factors in the external environment had an ad-
   verse impact on implementation (60 percent).

Other implementation problems include insufficient support for
change or unclear goals. Although implementation can be a tricky and
unpredictable challenge, you can improve the odds of success if you
enlist the support and involvement of key people, craft a solid plan,
support the plan with consistent behaviors, develop enabling structures, celebrate milestone successes, and communicate relentlessly.

Enlist the Support and
Involvement of Key People

Your implementation will go more smoothly if it has the backing
and involvement of key people—and not just the CEO and his or
her court. It is also critical to enlist managers and employees whom
others respect, individuals with key technical skills, people with access to vital resources, and the informal leaders to whom people naturally turn for direction and advice.

So how can you pinpoint these people? Authors Michael Tushman and Charles O'Reilly offer this advice:

> To determine who these key individuals are and what their responses to
> the change might be, ask: Who has the power to make or break the change?
> Who controls critical resources or expertise? Then think through how the
> change will likely affect each of these individuals and how each is likely
> to react toward the change. Who will gain or lose something. . . . Are
> there blocs of individuals likely to mobilize against or in support of the
> change effort?[2]

Enlisting support entails building an effective team of change
makers that can act together toward stated goals. But how can you be
sure you've picked the right people for the team? Here's a set of
questions that will help you know if your team has the right stuff:[3]

- Are enough of your company's key players (people in relevant
  positions of power) members of the team?

- Do members of the team have the relevant *expertise* to do the job and make intelligent decisions?

- Does the team include the needed *range* of perspectives and disciplines to do the job and make intelligent decisions?

- Does the team include people with sufficient credibility so that employees and management will treat its decisions seriously?

- Does the team include people with demonstrated leadership skills?

- Are the team members capable of forgoing their personal immediate interests in favor of the larger organizational goal?

If you answered "yes" to most of these questions, the team guiding the change effort is strong and in a good position to succeed. If you said "no" to any questions, it might be a good idea to revisit your team choices. (For more on selecting team members, see "Tips on Who Should *Not* Be on the Team.")

Craft an Implementation Plan

While a vision may guide and inspire team members during the change process, an organization also needs a nuts-and-bolts plan for what to do, and when and how to do it. This plan should map out the effort, specifying everything from where the first meetings should be held, to the date by which the company should reasonably expect to achieve its change goals. Here are some characteristics of a good implementation plan:[4]

- **It's simple.** An overly complex plan may confuse and frustrate participants in the change effort. So if your flowchart of activities and milestones looks like the wiring diagram for the space shuttle, rethink it with an eye toward simplicity and coherence.

- **It's created by people at all affected levels.** This goes back to Step 1 of the change process, which advocates "joint identification of business problems and their solutions." The implementation

Tips on Who Should Not Be on the Team

In his book on *Leading Change,* John Kotter recommends that you keep three types of people off your team:[a]

1. **People with big egos.** Big egos, per Kotter, fill the room, leaving little or no space for anybody else to participate or contribute. People with big egos don't always understand their own limitations and how those limitations can be complemented by the strength of others.

2. **Snakes.** Kotter describes a "snake" as the kind of person who secretly poisons relationships between team members. "A snake is an expert at telling Sally something about Fred and Fred something about Sally that undermines Sally and Fred's relationship."

3. **Reluctant players.** These are people who lack either the time or enthusiasm to provide energy to the team. Be wary of including these people on your team. Keeping them off may be difficult, however, since some reluctant players may have the expertise and/or organizational power you need.

[a]   John P. Kotter, *Leading Change* (Boston, MA: Harvard Business School Press, 1996), 59–61.

plan is part of the solution, and shouldn't be imposed on the people asked to push it forward. If the implementers and other people affected by the change are involved in making the plan, they'll be more enthusiastic in supporting the initiative. Remember, too, that a plan devised solely by strategists is less likely to reflect the realities of the business and what the organization can accomplish than a plan built on the ideas of the worker bees.

- **It's structured in achievable chunks.** Overly ambitious plans are usually doomed to failure. People look at them and say, "We'll never get this done—not in our lifetimes." They'll be defeated from the beginning. So build a plan that can be tackled in manageable, achievable segments.

- **It specifies roles and responsibilities.** Like every endeavor, a change plan should detail clear roles and responsibilities for everyone involved. Every planned outcome should be the acknowledged responsibility of one or more individuals. Those individuals should publicly state that they welcome and accept the responsibility. Input from all levels of the organization will help to achieve this role-oriented focus.

- **It's flexible.** As noted in the previous chapter, change programs seldom follow their planned trajectories or timetables. Thus, a good implementation plan is a living document open to revision. Organizations that lock themselves into rigid schedules, goals, and events, ultimately find themselves detached from the shifting world that surrounds them.

Support the Plan with Consistent Behaviors and Messages

Once the need for change has been articulated convincingly and broad support has been enlisted, that support must be maintained through a set of consistent behaviors and messages. Inconsistency in either will send a damaging message—that management is either not serious about implementing change or unwilling to do its part.

Consider this example: Not many years ago, one of the American Big Three automakers underwent a painful restructuring. Everyone was asked to sacrifice by giving up benefits today in order to achieve greater competitiveness and prosperity tomorrow. Thousands of middle managers and employees were laid off and the company's union was asked to forego pay and benefit increases. Because the company had made a convincing case for change, people got the message and tightened their belts; even the unions pitched in. Within months, however, senior management awarded itself and other key people bonuses and substantial pay increases. Once that inconsistent behavior became public, the bonds of trust between management and the rank and file—and their unions—evaporated. Collaboration turned to open hostility that simmered for nearly ten years.

At about the same time, a company in another industry was likewise supporting a belt-tightening and restructuring program. But this one did so with highly visible and consistent deeds. Its CEO set the pace by selling the corporation's three jets and taking commercial flights on his travels—in coach class to boot. And no more limos to meet him at the airport. "I don't mind taking a cab," he told the business press. "They can get me to where I'm going just as fast." The company's other traveling executives followed the lead of their boss. People noticed.

Which of these companies do you suppose was more successful in building support for its change program?

SQA, Herman Miller's successful low-cost office furniture unit, used a consistent set of messages to support its effort to increase on-time, accurate fulfillment of orders. Everyone understood that this was the unit's key measure of successful change. So SQA managers came up with several ways to reinforce that understanding. For example, they installed signboards at every entrance to the plant, and each morning they posted the previous day's percentage of on-time orders. It was impossible to enter or leave the plant without knowing the previous day's performance. They also added the on-time order metric to internal e-mail messages. "Yesterday's percentage of on-time accurately filled orders was 99.2%." The vice president of operations even adopted the practice of randomly asking employees if they knew the previous day's score. A correct answer was rewarded with either a crisp $100 bill or a paid day off.

What messages or behaviors would be consistent with the change program at your company?

Develop Enabling Structures

Enabling structures are the activities and programs that underpin successful implementation and are a critical part of the overall plan. Such structures include pilot programs, training, and reward systems.

Pilot programs give people opportunities to grapple with implementation and its problems on a smaller, more manageable scale. Pilots are test beds in which implementers can experiment with and de-bug change initiatives before rolling them out more broadly. These programs can be valuable proving ground since it's almost always easier and less risky to change a single department than an entire company.

Training programs can hold equal value. Motorola and General Electric developed formal training programs that served as key enablers for the ensuing quality initiatives. Xerox did the same when it set up its companywide benchmarking program in the mid-1980s. Every Xerox employee received a copy of "the little yellow book," as they called the company's how-to manual on benchmarking methods, and skilled trainers were placed in almost every operating unit of the company.

Reward systems also play an enabling role. People generally adopt behaviors that produce rewards, and abandon those that are unrewarded. Thus, if your change program asks people to either work harder, work smarter, or work in new ways, your reward system must be aligned with the desired behaviors. However, the details and pitfalls of crafting incentive programs are complex and situationally determined and thus need to be crafted within the context of each organization.

Celebrate Milestones

Change initiatives can be long and frustrating. But you can keep up peoples' spirits and energy if you identify milestones—even small ones—and celebrate them as they are achieved. (See "Tips for Celebrating Short-Term Wins.") Celebrating a series of short-term wins can:

- neutralize skepticism about the change effort;
- provide evidence that peoples' sacrifices and hard work are paying off;
- help retain the support of senior management;
- keep up the momentum; and
- boost morale.

Tips for Celebrating Short-Term Wins

Here are just a few ideas for celebrating short-term wins and keeping your team pumped up:

- Treat change participants to a catered lunch—and bring in an outside speaker who can talk about his or her company's success in doing something similar.

- Have a picnic.

- Take the afternoon off for a softball game.

- Recognize the deeds of exceptional contributors.

Do something grander for major successes. For example, when you've successfully reached the midpoint of the initiative, host a dinner with the CEO as guest and keynote speaker.

There is a fine line between celebrating a successful milestone and making a premature declaration of victory. Crossing it will dissipate the sense of urgency you need to keep people motivated and moving on toward future hurdles.

John Kotter, who lists "declaring victory too soon" among the reasons that transformation efforts fail, says that both change initiators and change resisters have reasons for making this mistake. "In their enthusiasm over a clear sign of progress," he writes, "the initiators go overboard. They are then joined by resistors, who are quick to spot any opportunity to stop change. . . . [T]he resistors point to the victory as a sign that the war has been won and the troops should be sent home."[5] Catastrophe follows if the weary troops accept this argument and go back to their usual activities.

So instead of declaring victory, use the credibility and momentum gained from your short-term win to muster an attack on the next milestone.

Communicate Relentlessly

Communication is an effective tool for motivating employees, for over-coming resistance to an initiative, for preparing people for the pluses and minuses of change, and for giving employees a personal stake in the process. Effective communication can set the tone for a change program and is critical to implementation from the very start. But don't rely on a single Big Bang announcement to keep employees in line with the effort. Communication must be ongoing. (See "Putting Communication to Work" for a story emphasizing the importance of ongoing communication.) Here are eleven tips for communicating during a change effort:[6]

1. **Specify the nature of the change.** Slogans, themes, and phrases don't define what the change is expected to achieve. Communi-cate specific information about how the change will affect cus-tomer satisfaction, quality, market share or sales, or productivity.

2. **Explain why.** Employees are often left in the dark about the business reasons behind the change. You may have spent lots of time studying the problem and digging out the facts, but your coworkers aren't privy to that information. In addition, share with employees the various options available and why some (or one) is better than the others.

3. **Explain the scope of the change, even if it contains bad news.** Some people are more affected by change projects than others. And that leads to lots of fear-generating speculation. Fear and uncertainty can paralyze a company. You can short-circuit fear and uncertainty with the facts. But don't sugarcoat them. If people will be laid off, be up front about it. Also explain the things that will *not* change. This will help anchor people.

4. **Develop a graphic representation of the change project that people can understand and hold in their heads.** It might be a flow chart of what must happen, or a graphic image of what the changed enterprise will look like. Whatever it is, keep it clear, simple, and memorable.

5. **Predict negative aspects of implementation.** There are bound to be negatives, and people should anticipate them.

6. **Explain the criteria for success and how it will be measured.** Define success clearly, and devise metrics for progress toward it. If you fail to establish clear measures for what you aim to accomplish, how would anyone know if they had moved forward? Measure progress as you move forward—and then communicate that progress.

7. **Explain how people will be rewarded for success.** People need incentive for the added work and disruptions that change requires. Be very clear about how individuals will be rewarded for progress toward change goals.

8. **Repeat, repeat, and repeat the purpose of change and actions planned.** If the initial announcement doesn't generate questions, do not assume that employees accept the need for change—they may simply be surprised, puzzled, or shocked. So follow up your initial announcement meeting with another meeting. Follow this with communications that address individual aspects of the change project.

9. **Use a diverse set of communication styles that is appropriate for the audience.** Successful change programs build communications into their plans, using dedicated newsletters, events, e-mails, and stand-up presentations to keep people informed, involved, and keyed up. These communications should be honest about successes and failures. If people lose trust in what they are hearing, they will tune you out.

10. **Make communication a two-way proposition.** Remember, this is a shared enterprise. So, if you are a change leader, spend at least as much time listening as telling. Your attention to this point will help keep others involved and motivated. Leaders need feedback, and the hardworking implementers need opportunities to share their learning and their concerns with leaders who listen.

11. **Be a poster–boy or poster–girl for the change program.** If you are the boss, people will have their eyes on you. They will listen to your words, but will also look for inconsistencies between your words and what you communicate through body language and behavior. Do you speak and act with genuine enthusiasm? Does your tone and manner signal confidence in the project, or do you appear to be going through the motions? Try to see yourself as others see you.

Using Consultants

We end this chapter on implementation with a brief discussion of the role of consultants, and how and when they can help you.

Consultants have been working with companies since the early

Putting Communication to Work

Communication played a big role in the successful change program that pulled Continental Airlines out of a nosedive in the 1990s. Here's how president and CEO Greg Brenneman described Continental's approach in an article for the *Harvard Business Review:*

When I arrived at Continental, it was a mean and lousy place to work. For years, different groups of employees had been pitted against one another in the effort to drive down labor costs. Management's implicit communication policy had been, Don't tell anybody anything unless absolutely required. As a result, most employees learned of the company's activities, plans, and performance through the press. Talk about sending a message about who matters and who doesn't.

On top of that, employees had no place to go with ideas or questions. There were forms for employees' suggestions on how to improve the operations, but the suggestions disappeared into a black

hole. Add to that the fact that corporate headquarters was locked up like Fort Knox: the president's secretary had a buzzer under her desk that she could use to summon the police.

Needless to say, morale was terrible. A couple of weeks after I arrived, I was walking the ramp in Houston saying hello to our mechanics and baggage handlers, and helping to throw a bag or two, when I noticed that almost all the employees had torn the Continental logos from their shirts. When I asked one mechanic why he had done this, he explained, "When I go to Wal-Mart tonight, I don't want anyone to know that I work for Continental." His response still sends chills down my spine.

Now, how to create a new culture is the topic of hundreds, if not thousands, of books and articles. But Gordon [Bethune] and I didn't bother with them. We agreed that a healthy culture is simply a function of several factors, namely: honesty, trust, dignity, and respect. They all go together; they reinforce one another. When they are constants in a business, people become engaged in their work. They care; they talk; they laugh. And then fun happens pretty naturally. But honesty and the rest don't just sprout up like weeds in a cornfield, especially when there has been a long drought. In a turnaround situation, people are tense and suspicious for good reason. They've been lied to. They've seen their friends get fired. They fear they will be next.

So cultivating honesty, trust, dignity, and respect becomes the job of the leaders. It may even be their most important job; Gordon and I certainly considered it our top priority. That's why when we took over, we started talking with employees at every opportunity. We got out there in the airports and on the planes. We loaded bags; we stood alongside the agents at ticket counters. We just talked at every opportunity about our plans for the airline and how we were going to accomplish them. In general, our communication policy changed from, Don't tell anybody anything unless absolutely required, to Tell everybody everything.

SOURCE: Greg Brenneman, "Right Away and All at Once: How We Saved Continental," *Harvard Business Review* 76, no. 5 (September–October 1998): 176.

post-World War II era, when McKinsey and Boston Consulting Group began offering strategic planning advice to corporate executives. But the real growth in management consulting came through human resource departments when academic work in the social/behavioral sciences—particularly in psychology, sociology, social anthropology, and organizational behavior—found applications (and paying customers) in the world of business. Indeed, many in the field of management consulting see themselves as conduits through which concepts developed in the academic realm can be tested and applied in the real world.

From those HR and training origins, consultants have developed new and more lucrative practices in the field of change management. During the early 1980s, the hottest cards in the deck were total quality management and its offspring: benchmarking, *kaisan,* and service excellence. A decade later process reengineering and organizational learning were the favored corporate elixirs. More recently, consulting companies have ridden a wave of interest in enterprise—linking information systems, and helping companies design, install, and eventually manage them.

Before enlisting the help of a consultant in your change initiative, it is important to understand how consultants can help you, and how you can make the most of their services (see appendix B for more information on selecting a consultant).

With respect to change initiatives it's useful to think of two types of consultants:

- **Expert consultants.** They help to shape the context of change. Which strategy needs to change? Which structure? Which systems?

- **Process consultants.** They recommend processes for making change happen, and help implement them. They also coach the leadership and the change team.

Either of these types of consultants augment the organization's official leadership and generally follow this modus operandi:

1. **Diagnosis.** A team of junior consultants gathers information both inside and outside the organization with the goal of:

1) determining where the company stands in terms of some measure of organization performance, and 2) the company's problems and the root causes with respect to that performance measure.

2. **Capabilities assessment.** The capabilities of the company's human and physical resources are assessed.

3. **Strategy development.** Working with management, the consulting team develops a strategy for reaching the desired level of performance. Depending on the situation, that strategy may include various doses of employee training, process reengineering, organizational restructuring, and even some new information technology.

4. **Implementation.** Consultant teams provide training and work with employee teams to plan the change program and operationalize the strategy.

From the organization's point of view, it is generally most useful to give consultants the lead with some of these agenda items and use them in advisory roles for others. For example, a consultant is often ideally suited to conduct agenda items 1 and 2. He or she can be more objective in making a diagnosis and assessing internal capabilities than can an internal team. Also, the consultant is likely to have an intimate knowledge of industry best practices that your own people may lack.

As you move through the agenda, consultants should gradually assume background roles. Beginning with the strategy development phase, company personnel have an obligation to shoulder more and more of the burden, as shown in figure 4-1. After all, it's their program, and they'll have to live with it.

The relationship we've described is, of course, a generalized model. Different types of programs will call for different roles and relationships. Consider the Theory E and Theory O approaches we described in chapter 1 of this book. As you may recall, Theory E change is a top-down approach that focuses on restructuring the asset base of the business with the goal of producing rapid improvements in shareholder value. Such change relies heavily on consultants, who

FIGURE 4 - 1

The Roles of Consultants and Employees in Change Programs

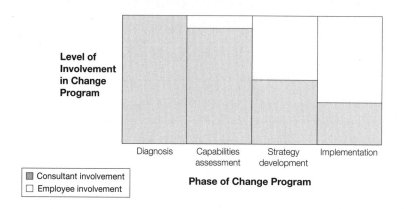

Consultant involvement
Employee involvement

Phase of Change Program

identify and analyze the problems and shape the solutions. According to authors Michael Beer and Nitin Nohria, "A SWAT team of Ivy League-educated MBAs, armed with an arsenal of state-of-the-art ideas, is brought in to find new ways to look at the business and manage it. The consultants can help CEOs get a fix on urgent issues and priorities. They also offer much-needed political and psychological support for CEOs who are under fire from financial markets."[7]

Theory O change programs, in contrast, rely far less on consultants. Instead, consultants act as expert resources who prepare and empower employees to do the heavy lifting of change, including business analysis and the crafting of solutions. This is, in effect, what happened in General Electric's famous "Work Out" initiative of the late 1980s —a prototypical Theory O change program. That program aimed to stamp out bureaucracy (which CEO Jack Welch loathed) and reshape the operating units to behave more like entrepreneurial small companies. Consultants had the job of organizing New England–style "town meetings" for each of the company's operating units. Small groups of employees were invited to these meetings, where consultants facilitated discussion between bosses and employees on how each group's business could be improved.

Thus, the best approach to using consultants is bound to be heavily situational. If the goal is restructuring, change consultants can and should play a major role—they have very specialized knowledge and experience for these rare events. But if the change involves changing how people work, put your own people in change and use consultants as facilitators.

Summing Up

This chapter addressed the all-important phase of implementation in a change program. Without effective implementation, all the front-end analysis, strategizing, and planning will be a waste of time and money.

Six activities were identified as essential for implementation:

1. **Enlisting the support and involvement of key people.** This means assembling a team with the right blend of skills, authority, resources, and leadership.

2. **Crafting a good implementation plan.** Remember to keep it simple, flexible, divided into achievable chunks, and with clearly defined roles and responsibilities.

3. **Supporting the plan with consistent behaviors.** Make sure that management "walks the talk."

4. **Developing "enabling structures."** This means training, pilot programs, and alignment of the rewards system with your change goals.

5. **Celebrating milestones.** Identify important milestones in the project and celebrate them when they are reached.

6. **Communicating relentlessly.** Tell them why, tell them how, and tell them often.

Do these well and you'll tilt the odds of success in your favor.

The role of consultants was also discussed in this chapter. Exactly how consultants should participate is generally a function of the type of change you're aiming for.

- If the change is restructuring, with the purchase, sale, and/or consolidation of units, consultants will play a large role.

- If the change involves how people work together, company personnel should be prepared to carry the burden of leadership.

Social and Human Factors

Reactions to Change

Key Topics Covered in This Chapter

- *The rank and file, and how they respond to change*

- *Change resisters, and how to deal with them*

- *Change agents—the people who can make things happen*

ORGANIZATIONS are inherently social systems. The people in these systems have identities, relationships, communities, attitudes, emotions, and differentiated powers. So when you try to change any part of the system, all of these factors come into play, adding many layers of complexity to a change process. Successful management of change requires that you recognize the primacy of people factors and the social systems in which they operate.

The rank and file, the resisters, and the change agents are the three sets of players typically encountered in a change initiative. Each has unique characteristics, and each requires a different style of management.

The Rank and File

If you've spent much time observing life in the forest, you've probably noticed how animals establish routines. Deer, for example, create paths between their daytime sleeping areas and the streams, fields, and meadows where they look for food and water after dark. They stick to those paths as long as they are safe and offer few impediments to movement.

People also develop routines. Think about your own routine on a typical Saturday morning. Sleep until 8. Start a load of laundry. Cook the nice breakfast you never have time to make during the week. Pay the week's bills. Take the dog for a walk to the park. Chances are that you have routines at work as well. Like the woodland deer, people follow trails that are familiar, comfortable, safe, and satisfying. And they aren't eager to change unless given compelling reasons to do so. People also have "social routines" at work—associations with coworkers that satisfy their needs as social animals—and changes that impinge on those routines are equally unwelcome.

Occasional diversions from routines and existing social patterns add variety and interest—which please us. But diversions may also create tension, anxiety, discomfort, and even fear. As the late long-shoreman-philosopher Eric Hoffer wrote in *The Ordeal of Change:* "It is my impression that no one really likes the new. We are afraid of it." He notes that even small changes from the routine can be upsetting.

> *Back in 1936 I spent a good part of the year picking peas. I started out early in January in the Imperial Valley [of California] and drifted north-ward, picking peas as they ripened, until I picked the last peas of the season in June, around Tracy. Then I shifted all the way to Lake County, where for the first time I was going to pick string beans. And I still re-member how hesitant I was that first morning as I was about to address myself to the string bean vines. Would I be able to pick string beans? Even the change from peas to string beans had in it elements of fear.*
>
> *In the case of drastic change the uneasiness is of course deeper and more lasting. We can never be really prepared for that which is wholly new. We have to adjust ourselves and every radical adjustment is a crisis in self-esteem: we undergo a test, we have to prove ourselves. It needs in-ordinate self-confidence to face drastic change without inner trembling.*[1]

Certainly no two people feel the same "trembling" described by Hoffer. And some individuals are absolutely energized by change. The Myers-Briggs personality framework addresses this broad spectrum. At one end of the spectrum, for example, it describes a person who likes a planned and organized approach to life (a "judging" person). He or she likes things settled. At the other end of the spectrum is the "perceiving" person who prefers open options and a flexible and spontaneous approach to life.[2] You probably have people representing both types in your organization, and as a manager, you need to learn to deal with the full range of personalities. In particular:

- Think about the people who will participate in your change initiative. Who will react negatively to having their routines disrupted, and who will positively enjoy the experience? Make a list.

- Once you've identified people likely to be uncomfortable with change, think about their roles in the change initiative. They probably aren't the ones you'll want in key positions where initiative and enthusiasm are needed. Think, too, about how these individuals can be helped through the process.

- For individuals with pro-change dispositions, consider ways to optimize the energy they bring to the program, and how they can work with others.

And don't forget about yourself. Like everyone else you have a unique disposition to change. You either love it, hate it, or (more likely) you're somewhere between those extremes.

Discovery Learning, Inc. of Greensboro, North Carolina, has developed a helpful methodology for measuring an individual's disposition to change, indicating where that person is likely to fall on a "preferred style" continuum.[3] In their model, "Conservers" occupy one end of the continuum. Conservers are people who prefer current circumstances over the unknown—people who are more comfortable with gradual change than with anything radical. Occupying the opposite end of the spectrum are the "Originators," who prefer more rapid and radical change. "Originators are representative of the reengineering approach to change," according to Discovery Learning. "The goal of an Originator is to challenge existing structure, resulting in fast, fundamentally different, even systemic changes."[4] Occupying a middle position between these two extremes are the "Pragmatists" who support change when it clearly addresses current challenges. Pragmatists are less wedded to the existing structure than to structures that are likely to be successful. (See "Change Style Characteristics" for more on how Discovery Learning generalizes the characteristics of people who represent these three change style preferences.)

Change Style Characteristics

When Facing Change, Conservers:

- Generally appear deliberate, disciplined, and organized

- Prefer change that maintains current structure

- May operate from conventional assumptions

- Enjoy predictability

- May appear cautious and inflexible

- May focus on details and the routine

- Honor tradition and established practice

When Facing Change, Pragmatists:

- May appear practical, agreeable, flexible

- Prefer change that emphasizes workable outcomes

- Are more focused on results than structure

- Operate as mediators and catalysts for understanding

- Are open to both sides of an argument

- May take more of a middle-of-the-road approach

- Appear more team-oriented

When Facing Change, Originators:

- May appear unorganized, undisciplined, unconventional, and spontaneous

- Prefer change that challenges current structure

Continued

- Will likely challenge accepted assumptions

- Enjoy risk and uncertainty

- May be impractical and miss important details

- May appear as visionary and systemic in their thinking

- Can treat accepted policies and procedures with little regard

SOURCE: W. Christopher Musselwhite and Robyn Ingram, *Change Style Indicator* (Greensboro, NC: The Discovery Learning Press, 1999), 5–7. Used with permission.

Knowing where your coworkers stand—and where you stand—in a change preference continuum such as this one can help you be more effective in managing the people side of a change initiative.

The Resisters

"The reformer has enemies in all those who profit by the old order," Machiavelli warned his readers. And what held true in sixteenth-century Italy remains true today. Some people clearly enjoy advantages that—rightly or wrongly—they view as threatened by change. They may perceive change as endangering their livelihoods, their perks, their workplace social arrangements, or their status in the organization. Others know that their specialized skills will be rendered less valuable. For example, when a supplier of automotive hydraulic steering systems switched in the late 1990s to electronic steering technology, employees with expertise in hoses, valves, and fluid pressure were suddenly less important. The know-how they had developed over long careers was suddenly less valuable for the company.

Any time people perceive themselves as losers in a change initiative, expect resistance. Resistance may be passive, in the form of non-commitment to the goals and the process for reaching them, or active, in the form of direct opposition or subversion. How will you deal with that resistance?

Change masters have dealt with resisters in different ways over the years. French revolutionaries used the guillotine. The Bolsheviks had resisters shot or packed off to the gulags. Mao and his communist followers sent them to "reeducation" camps. Employment laws have removed these proven techniques from the corporate change master's tool kit, but there are other things you can do. You can begin by identifying potential resisters and try to redirect them. Here's where you can start:

- Always try to answer the question, "Where and how will change create pain or loss in the organization?"

- Identify people who have something to lose, and try to anticipate how they will respond.

- Communicate the "why" of change to potential resisters. Explain the urgency of moving away from established routines or arrangements.

- Emphasize the benefits of change to potential resisters. Those benefits might be greater future job security, higher pay, and so forth. There's no guarantee that the benefits of change will exceed the losses for these individuals. However, explaining the benefits will help shift their focus from negatives to positives.

- Help resisters find new roles—roles that represent genuine contributions *and* mitigate their losses.

- Remember that many people resist change because it represents a loss of control over their daily lives. You can return some of that control by making them active partners in the change program.

If these interventions fail, move resisters out of your unit. You cannot afford to let a few disgruntled individuals subvert the progress of the entire group. But don't make them "walk the plank." Do what you can to relocate them to positions where their particular skills can be better used. That's what the innovator of electronic steering systems did. That company still had plenty of business supplying hydraulic systems to car and truck manufacturers, so it employed its hydraulic specialists in those units even as it hired electronic engineers for its expanding new business.

As you consider resisters, don't forget that your own approach to initiating or managing change may be contributing to the problem. We noted in the previous chapter that "technical" solutions imposed from the outside often breed resistance because they fail to recognize the social dimension of work. Paul Lawrence made this point many years ago in his classic *Harvard Business Review* article "How to Deal With Resistance to Change."[5] In looking at interrelationships among employees Lawrence found that change originating among employees who work closely together is usually implemented smoothly. But change imposed by outsiders threatens powerful social bonds, generating resentment and resistance. So be sure to evaluate what part you may be playing in the resistance problem.

Dealing with Passive Resisters

Earlier, we described passive resistance to change as noncommitment to goals and the process for reaching them. Passive resisters frustrate managers. While they don't sabotage the program, they certainly don't help the initiative move forward.

The reason that a person won't change, explain psychologists Robert Kegan and Lisa Laskow Lahey, is that he or she has a "competing commitment"—a subconscious, hidden goal that conflicts with the *stated* commitment.[6] For example, a project leader who is dragging his feet may have an unrecognized competing commitment to avoid tougher assignments that may come his way if he's too successful with the current project. A supervisor who cannot seem to get on board with the new team-based approach to problem-solving may be worried that she will be seen as incompetent if she cannot solve problems herself.

Though competing commitments are likely to be lodged deep in an employee's psyche, some serious probing on your part can sometimes get them to the surface, where you and the employee can deal with them. The most practical advice here is to engage in one-on-one communication with the passive resister. You need to find out what's keeping this person from participating in an active way.

The Change Agents

Think for a moment about the big, big changes in the world over the centuries. Chances are that you can associate individuals with each of those changes. Copernicus and Galileo ultimately changed our view of where we stand relative to our neighbors in the solar system. Martin Luther split Christendom in two and contributed indirectly to the rise of nation states in Europe. Charles Darwin's theory on natural selection torpedoed the accepted wisdom on humankind's history. Karl Marx, a thinker, and Vladimir Lenin, a doer, created a communist movement that, at its apex, held sway over almost half the world. Henry Ford and his engineers developed a new approach to manufacturing—the assembly line—that fundamentally altered the auto industry and many other industries. In each of these cases, someone who thought differently had a major impact on human history. None began with serious resources or backing, all were outsiders, and all faced substantial opposition. All were what we call *change agents*.

Change agents are catalysts who get the ball rolling, even if they do not necessarily do most of the pushing. Everett Rogers described them as figures with one foot in the old world and one in the new— creators of a bridge across which others can travel.[7] They help others to see what the problems are, and convince them to grapple with them. Change agents, in his view, fulfill critical roles. They:

- articulate the need for change;

- are accepted by others as trustworthy and competent (people must accept the messenger before they accept the message);

- see and diagnose problems from the perspective of their audience;

- motivate people to change;

- work through others in translating intent into action;

- stabilize the adoption of innovation; and

- foster self-renewing behavior in others so that they can "go out of business" as change agents.

Who in your organization has these characteristics? Are you one of them? It is important to identify the change agents so that you can place them in key positions during a change effort. In a self-regenerating company, you'll find change agents in many different operating units and at all different levels. (See "Tips for Identifying Change Agents" for more information.)

Can change agents be created? Perhaps. One German electronics firm did so in the 1990s when it faced poor financial performance, sagging morale, and weak competitiveness. The company was over-consulted and under-managed. Many of its best young employees were unhappy with consecutive years of losses and dimming prospects. The company's rigid corporate hierarchy was partly to blame. Management recognized that it had to distribute authority and decision making more broadly. To accomplish this it created a change agent program that sent two dozen hand-picked employees to the United States for special training, which included abundant exposure to entrepreneurial American firms. Once the training program was completed, the newly minted change agents were transferred back to their units, where they worked to break the mold of the old hierarchical system.

General Motors attempted something very similar in its joint venture with Toyota: the NUMMI small car assembly plant in California. That plant was run according to Toyota's world-beating production methods, and GM rotated manufacturing managers through the plant to learn Toyota's methods and, hopefully, bring a working knowledge of those methods back to Detroit. As described earlier, furniture maker Herman Miller sought the same result when it moved managers from its SQA unit into its traditional operating units; it figured that these individuals would infect others with their faster, more accurate approach to manufacturing and fulfillment.

Your search for change agents shouldn't necessarily be limited to company personnel. Every so often it's wise to look outside for people who have the skills and attitudes required to stir things up and get the organization moving in a new and more promising direction. This approach is not without risk, since the outsider's lack of familiarity with the company's culture may result in unforeseen turmoil. For a discussion of this issue, see "The Insider-Outsider as Change Agent" and its *Harvard Business Review* excerpt.

Tips for Identifying Change Agents

- Find out who people listen to. Change agents lead with the power of their ideas. But be warned: These may not be employees with formal authority to lead.

- Be alert to people who "think otherwise." Change agents are not satisfied with things as they are—a fact that may not endear them to management.

- Take a close look at new employees who have come from outside the circle of traditional competitors. They may not be infected with the same mind-set as everyone else.

- Look for people with unusual training or experience. For example, if all your marketing people have business degrees and heavy quantitative research backgrounds, look for the oddball liberal arts major who has a degree in social anthropology. Chances are she sees the world through a different lens.

The Insider-Outsider as Change Agent

Many companies feel that the only way to create change and make it stick is to bring in outsiders with no ties to the status quo. Others fear that outsiders who don't understand the business, its culture, and its values will simply create disruption. Writing in the *Harvard Business Review*, Donald Sull recommends that leadership for change be invested in individuals who represent both sides of the coin: a fresh perspective on the business *and* a solid appreciation for the company's culture.

Guiding a company through big changes requires a difficult balancing act. The company's heritage has to be respected even as it's being resisted. It's often assumed that outsider managers are best suited to lead such an effort since they're not bound by the company's historical

Continued

formula. . . . Typically, outsiders are so quick to throw out all the old ways of working that they end up doing more harm than good.

The approach I recommend is to look for new leaders from within the company but from outside the core business. These managers, whom I call inside-outsiders, can be drawn from the company's smaller divisions, from international operations, or from staff functions. . . .

Insider-outsiders have led many of the most dramatic corporate transformations in recent times. Jack Welch spent most of his career in GE's plastics business; Jürgen Schrempp was posted in South Africa before returning to run [DaimlerChrysler]; and Domenico De Sole served as the Gucci Group's legal counsel before leading that company's dramatic rejuvenation.

Another alternative is to assemble management teams that leverage the strengths of both insiders and outsiders. When [Lou] Gerstner took over at IBM, he didn't force out all the old guard. Most operating positions continued to be staffed by IBM veterans with decades of experience, but they were supported by outsiders in key staff slots and marketing roles. The combination of perspectives has allowed IBM to use old strengths to fuel its passage down an entirely new course.

Finally, inside managers can break free of their old formulas by imagining themselves as outsiders, as Intel's executives did in deciding to abandon the memory business. Intel had pioneered the market for memory chips, and for most of its executives, employees, and customers, Intel meant memory. As new competitors entered the market, however, Intel saw its share of the memory business dwindle. . . .

Although Intel had built an attractive microprocessor business during this time, it clung to the memory business until its chairman, Gordon Moore, and its president, Andy Grove, sat down and deliberately imagined what would happen if they were replaced with outsiders. They agreed that outsiders would get out of the memory business—and that's exactly what Moore and Grove did. While a company's competitive formula exerts a tremendous gravitational pull, thinking like outsiders can help insiders to break free.[a]

---

[a] Donald N. Sull, "Why Good Companies Go Bad," *Harvard Business Review* 77, no. 4 (July–August 1999): 50.

Summing Up

Change is complicated by the fact that organizations are social systems whose participants have identities, relationships, communities, routines, emotions, and differentiated powers. Thus managers must be alert to how a change will conflict with existing social systems and individual routines.

This chapter explored the three identity categories that employees typically fall into:

- The *rank and file* is likely to include people who exhibit a spectrum of reactions to change. This chapter adopted the terms "conservers," "pragmatists," and "originators" to describe how different people respond to change. Knowing where your coworkers stand—and where you stand—in a change preference continuum such as this one can help you be more effective in managing the people side of a change initiative.

- *Change resisters* will either drag their feet or actively attempt to undermine your efforts. You can identify potential resisters by determining where and how change will create pain or loss in the organization. Once you've identified them, there are several things you can do to neutralize their resistance or make them active participants. These include: explaining the urgent need to change, describing how change will produce benefits for them, and finding new ways in which they can contribute. People who do not respond to these efforts should be moved out of your unit.

- *Change agents* see the need for change and articulate it effectively to others. They are critical catalysts for a change initiative and should be placed in key positions. This chapter has provided tips for identifying change agents.

6

Helping People Adapt

Strategies to Help Reduce Stress and Anxiety

Key Topics Covered in This Chapter

- *The four stages of reaction to change: shock, defensive retreat, acknowledgment, and acceptance and adaptation*

- *How individuals can help themselves navigate change*

- *How managers can help employees cope with change*

- *Alternative ways for managers to think about change resisters*

THE BUSINESS PRESS and many academics like to talk about the importance of change, and how it makes us all better people and more satisfied and fulfilled with our work. They extol the virtues of "thriving" on chaos and encourage us to "embrace" change as if it were something we just can't get enough of. You get the feeling that had they been around during the thirteenth century these writers would have described the Crusaders' sack of Constantinople as a "mutual learning experience" for the Latin West and the Byzantine East.

In reality, change puts lots of people through the wringer—particularly Theory E change that aims to quickly increase shareholder value. Far from "thriving," some employees don't survive the change program at all, let alone come out in one piece. Both unsuccessful and successful change programs produce stress, and many result in the displacement of good people. Ask the thousands of General Electric employees who lost their jobs when Jack Welch pared down his company to a manageable set of future-facing businesses. They didn't call him Neutron Jack for nothing. The same goes for "Chainsaw" Al Dunlap, who lopped off great chunks of the employment ranks at Scott Paper in a major corporate makeover. Ask the people who survived several rounds of downsizing at IBM and Cisco Systems about "embracing" change.

In these types of changes, survivors are almost universally shell-shocked. Their morale is poor, trust in the company is at rock bottom, and employee loyalty is out the window. A good manager cannot restore the world for these people, but he or she can help them through the turmoil, and get them back into a productive frame of mind. This chapter explains the stress caused by workplace change and what you can do to help people through it.

Reactions to Change: A Sense of Loss and Anxiety

The typical employee spends at least eight hours a day doing, in general, fairly routine tasks. Indeed, when companies talk about their "culture," they imply a certain measure of stability and routine. They reinforce that stability with job descriptions that prescribe in concrete terms what employees should do day-to-day and week-to-week. There's a tangible agreement that if the employee does X, and does it well and on time, the employee will receive Y in compensation and be viewed as a company member in good standing.

There is also a psychological contract between employee and company: As long as the employee fits into work and social patterns, he or she "belongs." And there is a political dimension as well, demanding that career-minded employees attend to certain written and unwritten "rules" of the game. But what happens when the contract or rules are changed unexpectedly? Take the following case, for example:

> *This morning we got a memo addressed to "all staff." It said that year-end performance bonuses are being discontinued. Just like that—20 percent of my salary out the window! And after all the long hours I've put in during the last months. . . .*

How would you suppose this person might feel? She has definitely experienced a loss. Losses caused by change programs usually aren't as drastic as this, however. They are more likely to be a change in job description, or a perceived loss in turf, status, or self-meaning. They tend to be threats to values that someone has built up, rather than monetary losses.

Even a positive change can create anxiety for some people. For example, a person who's given a promotion may wonder: Can I handle the job? How will my friendships with people in the department be affected now that I'm their boss? Will the required travel and longer hours create problems at home?

Those questions reflect a fear of the unknown, which often accompanies a loss of certainty. For most people, however, the negative aspects of change are related to a loss of control—over their incomes and influence, their sources of pride, and how they have grown accustomed to living and working. When these factors are threatened, expect to see anxiety and anger.

Stages in Reaction to Change

Most people eventually adapt and are reconciled to change, but not before passing through various psychological stages, which are examined here. One way to think about those stages is through the concept of risk. According to one theory, change requires people to perform or perceive in unfamiliar ways, which involves risks. Those risks potentially threaten a person's self-esteem.[1] Understandably, people are uncomfortable with risk and tend to avoid it when they can. When they cannot, however—as when they're roped into a corporate change initiative—adaptation to change tends to proceed through predictable psychological stages. In some respects, these stages resemble the grieving process a person experiences after the loss of a loved one. The four stages are:[2]

1. **Shock.** In the shock phase, people feel threatened by antici- pated change. They may even deny its existence: "This isn't happening." They become immobilized and often shut down in order to protect themselves. People feel unsafe, timid, and unable to act, much less take risks. Needless to say, productivity drops during this stage.

2. **Defensive retreat.** Eventually people caught in a change vortex move from shock to defensive retreat. They get angry and lash out at what has been done to them, even as they hold on to accustomed ways of doing things. They attempt to keep a grip on the past

while decrying the fact that it's changed. This conflict likewise precludes taking risks; the situation is perceived as too unsafe.

3. **Acknowledgment.** Eventually, most people cease denying the fact of change, and acknowledge that they have lost something. They mourn. The psychological dynamics of this stage include both grief and liberation. Thus, one can feel like a pawn in a game while also being able to view that game with some degree of objectivity and psychological distance. At this point the notion of taking risks becomes more palatable and people begin to explore the pros and cons of the new situation. Each "risk" that succeeds builds confidence and prepares people for more.

4. **Acceptance and adaptation.** Most people eventually internalize the change, make any needed adaptations, and move on. They see themselves "before and after" the change and, even if it's a grudging acknowledgment, they consider the change "for the best." In some cases, people actively advocate for what they had previously opposed. Acceptance and adaptation means relinquishing the old situation, as well as the pain, confusion, and fear experienced in the earlier stages of change.

Progress through these four stages is linear and should only be accelerated with great care. Speeding up the process risks carrying unfinished psychological "baggage" from one phase to the next. Thus, if you're the manager of people going through the four-stage process you need to resist your natural bias toward action and exercise patience. The expression "time heals all" says it well enough.

This theory about how people deal with change and eventually accept it is somewhat simplistic. Although most people work through the four emotional stages—some more quickly than others—some will get stuck in defensive retreat and channel their energies into resistance.

People get stuck for two basic and obvious reasons: first, change is not a single event with neat and tidy beginnings and endings; and second, people's experiences with change vary with individual circumstance. Thus, frameworks like this one are far from perfect. To further complicate matters, change often hits from two or more directions at the same time. For example, a division of a large corporation is put through a wrenching restructuring in which many people are furloughed; the same division is then sold to another corporation, which results in new leadership and new policies. Coming all at once (or in rapid sequence), these multiple changes can severely stress or undo the anchor points of the employees and managers who remain. Agreed-upon ways of working, affiliations, skills, and self-concept slip away. When anchor points such as these are removed, most people are immobilized or thrown into a defense mode. In a worst-case scenario, the individual under siege at the office is simultaneously experiencing major change at home—a divorce, for example.

People who are emotionally fragile are at the greatest risk during change initiatives. They typically have the greatest difficulty handling feelings of loss and may choose to see themselves as victims of the process. A perception of victimhood will always hinder an employee's ability to move on after change has occurred.

The Conventional Advice

Smart managers attempt to accelerate adaptation to change, and for understandable reasons: Employees who are preoccupied with their internal issues are not fully productive. Indeed, people in the early stages of change are often unable to do much at all. It thus makes good business sense to help them cope and move forward. Unfortunately, such good intentions are often viewed as manipulative, controlling, or autocratic. If the benefits of change are overly hyped, if there are too many pep rallies and too many "it's really good for you" assurances, people will become cynical and dig in their heels. "How can they say everything is rosy when I feel as though I've been stabbed in the back?"

So, what can you do to minimize the negative aspects of change for people in your organization? Consider the following list of conventional advice for dealing with change:

- Keep your cool in dealing with others.

- Do your best to handle pressure smoothly and effectively.

- Respond nondefensively when others disagree with you.

- Develop creative and innovative solutions to problems.

- Be willing to take risks and try out new ideas.

- Be willing to adjust priorities to changing conditions.

- Demonstrate enthusiasm for and commitment to long-term goals.

- Be open and candid when dealing with others.

- Participate actively in the change process.

- Make clear-cut decisions as needed.

This is good advice, but it fails to take into account psychological needs that must be addressed. Most people are aware of the wisdom of taking responsibility for dealing with change themselves; they recognize the importance of the "right attitude." Most people, however, do not want this shoved down their throats. Rather, they prefer some empathy, and some understanding of what they are experiencing. They are less interested in advice than in understanding and support.

The next two sections explore ways in which people facing change can help themselves and provide guidelines that managers can use to help their employees (and themselves) cope with difficult parts of the change process.

What Individuals Can Do for Themselves

The strong emotions that most of us feel at the onset of change—anger, depression, and shock—are not useful. They neither comfort us nor move us forward. And they are often emotional. We have rational *and* emotional sides of our beings, and each must be paid its

Tips for Recognizing the Emotional Side

- Remind people that anger, depression, and shock are natural reactions to loss. People need to give themselves permission to feel what they are feeling. Change always involves a loss of some kind: a job, colleagues, a role, even one's identity. That loss must be duly acknowledged and mourned.

- Let mourning take its course.

- Be patient. Recognize that time is needed to come to grips with a situation and move through the various stages. It cannot be done overnight, and no single timeline works for everyone. But don't let people wallow in self-pity and grief.

due. (See "Tips for Recognizing the Emotional Side.") The secret to success is to allow the emotional side to express itself—that is, to give it due recognition—but to gradually pass control to the rational side.

Overcome Powerlessness

A feeling of powerlessness, or loss of control, is a major cause of change-related distress. Someone over whom we have no control has arbitrarily upset the routines of work, sold off the division, laid off many of our workplace friends, or altered the compensation system. Worse, we have no recourse.

One antidote to feeling powerless is to establish a sense of personal control in other areas of our lives. For example, taking charge of your investment club's monthly newsletter or designing a room addition to your house represent ways to regain a sense of personal control. Another antidote is to avoid taking on other efforts that sap energy. Thus, if adapting to change is arduous, individuals should husband their resources. This entails not only maintaining physical well-being, but nourishing your psyche. For example:

- get enough sleep

- pay attention to diet and exercise

- take occasional breaks at the office

- relax with friends

- engage in hobbies

These are not forms of escapism, nor do they distract a person from reality. Rather, they are practical ways of exerting control over one's life during a period of flux.

Inventory the Gains and Losses

Accepting strong emotions and acknowledging the importance of patience in dealing with change are vital; but so is developing objectivity about what is happening. We have choices in how we perceive change, and we are able to develop the capacity to see benefits, not just losses, in new situations. Coming to accept and adapt to change is in fact a process of balancing: "What have I lost?" should be balanced by "What am I gaining?" This is far different than "looking on the bright side." Inventorying personal losses and gains is a tangible step that people can take in gathering the strength to move on.

Re-anchor

"Re-anchoring" is related to inventorying gains and losses. Here, the individual balances the emotional investment in essential work-related anchor points—how work is done, affiliations, skills, self-concept in relation to the work—with emotional investments in other areas, such as family, friends, and civic and religious activities. Thus, when one or more anchor points at the workplace is uprooted, the person can remain steady by creating or strengthening anchor points elsewhere. For example, if workplace change has resulted in your transfer to a new department where you have no real friends, you could:

- develop new friendships in that department;

- join the department softball team; or

- solidify your friendships outside work—for example, by attending the Thursday night book club meeting you've skipped for the past year.

Admittedly, inventorying and re-anchoring are difficult when a person is in the grip of strong emotions. Perhaps the best mechanism for coping with change, then, is anticipating it. No one escapes the effects of change, in the workplace or elsewhere, but those who recognize that its impact will be powerful, that the process of adaptation and acceptance will take time, and that we all have other sources of strength, are much better positioned than those who are caught flat-footed.

How Managers Can Help Employees Cope

Many managers find that addressing straightforward, technical issues in the change effort—such as the new department layout, or who gets what training—is comparatively easy. But consciously or not, they ignore the more complex and unpredictable concerns of people being changed. The rationale may be a business one: "We don't have time for that; we're here to make money." Or it may be emotional: "I don't want to get involved in messy feelings; that's not my job."

Ignoring the human side of change, however, is shortsighted and a symptom of ineffective management. Managers are paid to get things done with the human and financial resources given to them— imperfect as those resources may be. Like infantry platoon leaders in a skirmish, they must muster all the firepower at their disposal—and that means getting every one of their people engaged. They cannot afford to write off people who are too afraid to move. They have to get everyone into the fight. And that sometimes means helping them through their fear. With that thought in mind, let's consider what managers can do at each of the four stages described earlier.

Stage One: Shock

Good managers prepare people for change long before the shock hits. Returning to our military example, military organizations don't wait until the heat of battle to deal with the shock it induces in people. Instead, they prepare soldiers for what lies ahead through rigorous training and simulations. As a manager, you, too, can prepare your people for the shock of change by periodically inoculating them with small doses of it:

- Change work processes whenever you see real opportunities for improvement.

- Give people periodic reassignments that force them to learn new things and deal with new situations.

- Use stretch goals to encourage flexibility and greater effort.

- Never allow anyone to get too comfortable in his or her job.

- Root out any sense of entitlement.

If you prepare people for change, they will experience less shock when a really big shake-up hits your unit. Preparation is probably the most important thing you can do as a change manager. Even with good preparation, however, there's bound to be shock, and you'll have to deal with the denial, "shutting down," and timidity that characterize this stage. You'll need to apply some "first aid":

- If people have had the anchors of their work lives yanked away, find new ones for them to latch onto. These may be their new roles in their new work groups.

- Provide opportunities for people to vent their feelings.

- Be a good listener, but avoid trying to sell them on the idea that things are actually better for them—they are not yet ready to hear this.

- Help your employees manage the stress that results from change (see the "Managing Stress Levels" checklist in appendix A).

Stage Two: Defensive Retreat

People in the stage of defensive retreat get angry and lash out even as they try to hold on to the old ways of doing things. This behavior reduces their productivity. Here are a couple things you can do to get them through this stage:

- Do what you can to keep "retreaters" connected to the immediate group—the strongest anchor there is. Individuals who find themselves decoupled from their familiar social arrangements are likely to be the most damaged, since the group acts as a source of identity, safety, and support. The military, which has enormous experience in this area, emphasizes what it calls "small group cohesion." It knows that soldiers will do remarkable things as members of small, closely-knit groups (see "The Power of Small Group Cohesion"). You should do the same by helping people connect to others in their new circumstances. Group activities, lunchtime meetings, or outings all help build connections between strangers.

- Provide a verbal outlet for the grievances and the angst that needs to be vented. When management provides opportunities for grievances and frustrations to be aired constructively, employee bitterness and frustration may be diminished.

Stage Three: Acknowledgment

Eventually, most people stop denying the fact of change and acknowledge their new situation. The psychological dynamics of this stage include both grief for what has been lost and nascent feelings of liberation. Though they continue to feel like pawns in a game controlled by others, they begin to view that game with a certain amount of distance and objectivity. Risk-taking becomes possible as people begin to explore the pros and cons of the new situation.

You can help people in this stage in several ways:

The Power of Small Group Cohesion

Biographer/historian William Manchester was wounded during the bloody World War II battle to take the Japanese-held island of Okinawa. Although Manchester had a "ticket home" wound, he skipped out of the field hospital and rejoined his unit of U.S. Marines, who were still in the thick of combat. Many years later he recollected the motivation that propelled him to put his life on the line (again). His account underscores the power of small group cohesion—something that every change manager must appreciate:

And then, in one of those great thundering jolts in which a man's real motives are revealed to him in an electrifying vision, I understand, at last, why I jumped hospital that Sunday thirty-five years ago, and, in violation of orders, returned to the front and almost certain death. It was an act of love. Those men on the line were my family, my home. . . . They had never let me down, and I couldn't do it to them. I had to be with them rather than to let them die and me live with the knowledge that I might have saved them. Men, I now knew, do not fight for flag or country, for the Marine Corps or glory or any other abstraction. They fight for one another.[a]

[a] William Manchester, *Goodbye Darkness* (Boston, MA: Little, Brown and Company, 1979).

- Continue your role as a sounding board for complaints and questions. Ask "How do you feel about this?" to get a fix on an individual's emotional state. But begin now to stress the benefits of the new situation.

- Build further on the "anchors" and group cohesion you established in the previous stage.

- Encourage people to try new things—to take some risks. Ask "What could we do about this?" Each risk that succeeds will build confidence and prepare people for the final stage.

Stage Four: Acceptance and Adaptation

Most employees will eventually accept their new situation and adapt to it. Others may drift off to new jobs they find more satisfactory—either inside or outside the organization. A certain number will never adapt, however, and their performance will suffer. Here are some things you can do to facilitate this final stage:

- Keep working on group dynamics. Remember that people are generally less concerned with the tasks they are given than how they fit in with the group.

- Try to understand what each of your people needs to feel a sense of accomplishment. For one person that might be an opportunity to demonstrate her special talent for creating PowerPoint presentations. For another it could be his project management ability. For each person, find that special talent and give him or her an opportunity to use it and to earn some recognition.

- Move the focus from feelings to action. Action will take their minds off their hurt feelings and insecurity, which will eventually fade away.

- Be prepared to "outplace" those individuals who simply cannot or will not fit into the new situation. These individuals will be a permanent drag on performance and cast a negative pall over the unit.

The advice given here about listening, accepting, and supporting may seem overly simple and obvious. But it's these simple and obvious actions that change managers often overlook. Don't make the same mistake. (For an inspirational story on how one leader managed change under stressful circumstances, see "How Shackleton Did It.")

Rethinking Resisters

Although addressed in a previous chapter, we return to the issue of change resistance here since such resistance is a natural human response—one with which managers must learn to cope.

"Resister" typically describes anyone who refuses to accept the change, or who doesn't change as fast as we do. As such, a resister is considered an obstacle to be overcome. Those labeled resisters are viewed as people with poor attitudes, or lacking in team spirit. But treating resisters this way serves only to intensify real resistance, thereby thwarting or at least sidetracking the possibility of change.

Resistance is a part of the natural process of adaptation to change—a normal response of those who have a strong interest in maintaining the current state and guarding themselves against loss. "Why should I give up what has created meaning for me?" they ask. "What do I get in its place?"

Resistance is generally more complicated than "I won't." It is a much more painful question: "Why should I?" Once resistance is understood as a natural reaction—part of a process—it can be viewed more objectively as a step in the process that leads to acceptance and adaptation. At the very minimum, resistance denotes energy—energy that can be worked with and redirected. The strength of resistance, moreover, indicates the degree to which change has touched on something valuable to an individual or the overall organization. Discovering what that valuable something is can help you manage the change effort. One theorist puts it this way:

> First, [the resisters] are the ones most apt to perceive and point out real threats, if such exist, to the well-being of the system, which may be the unanticipated consequences of projected changes. Second, they are especially apt to react against any change that might reduce the integrity of the system. Third, they are sensitive to any indication that those seeking change fail to understand or identify with the core values of the system they seek to influence.[3]

Thus, resisters may provide important information, and dismissing them as naysayers may be a genuine error.

In summary, rethinking resistance to change means seeing it as a normal part of adaptation, something most of us do to protect ourselves. It is a potential source of energy, as well as information about the change effort and direction. So, instead of viewing all resistance as an obstacle, try to understand its sources, motives, and potentially affirmative core. Doing so can open up possibilities for realizing change.

How Shackleton Did It

Thanks to many books and films produced over the past few years, most readers are probably familiar with the ill-fated Antarctic expedition of Sir Ernest Shackleton and his ship, *Endurance*. Though he utterly failed to accomplish his intended goal, Shackleton's success in holding his crew together, and in returning all to safety, has made him quite a hero. Much can be learned from his management and leadership in that period of extreme adversity.

The *Endurance* left England in 1914 with the goal of landing on the Antarctic shore and sending a team of men and dogs to the other side of the continent by way of the Pole—a feat that had not yet been accomplished. But Shackleton never made it to the staging area. Trapped by an ice pack in the Weddell Sea and unable to move, ship and crew were forced to stay put for almost fifteen months until the ice broke up. How Shackleton held his team together and kept them alive and healthy during that time in the world's most inhospitable environment provides insights into change management.

Like employees in a change situation over which they had no control, the *Endurance* crew saw that the goal they had enlisted for was abandoned. Everything they had hoped for and had prepared for had to be scratched. They were out of communication with the world they knew and could expect neither help nor rescue from any quarter. When the pressures of the ice eventually crushed the sides of the ship, slow starvation or death from exposure became highly probable.

How did their leader keep the expedition's members from mentally and physically shutting down under these circumstances? Here are three actions taken by Shackleton that proved effective:

- **He immediately provided a new and acceptable goal.** The crew would live on the ice pack until it broke up; they would then navigate to safety via the ship's lifeboats. As long as people had a worthy goal to work toward, their energies and spirits were maintained.

- **He kept everyone busy.** Fifteen months on an ice floe could have driven the crew to fratricide. So Shackleton made sure that everyone kept busy. Meteorological data was recorded daily. Regular soccer matches and dogsled races between teams supported group cohesion and maintained mental and physical health. A drama group was created to perform theatrical entertainment. Until the ship was eventually crushed, crewmembers tended to necessary repairs. A core team planned for the eventual voyage by lifeboat. Holidays were celebrated.

- **Difficult and undesirable chores were equally shared.** Shackleton, the ship's captain, and other leaders lived and worked with everyone else. There was no sense of "them" and "us." They were in it together.

In April, 1916, the ice floe on which the crew had survived for more than a year began to break apart. Lifeboats crammed with men and supplies were launched into the frigid sea—the first leg of a long and harrowing journey toward safety. And despite months of continued hardship and peril, every member of the Shackleton expedition survived and—together—returned safely to England.

Summing Up

This chapter described how people react to change and how managers can effectively deal with negative reactions. Here are some key points to remember:

- People faced with dramatic change generally respond through four stages: shock, defensive retreat, acknowledgment, and acceptance and adaptation. These stages are similar to the grieving process that follows the loss of a friend or family member. Your challenge as a change manager is to patiently help people through these stages.

- Individuals can overcome some of the emotional problems associated with change by: overcoming the powerlessness they feel
  by developing a sense of personal control over other areas of
  their lives; gaining greater objectivity of their situations by making an inventory of personal losses and gains; and "re-anchoring"
  themselves.

- Managers can help people through the four stages using a number of methods, which include listening, keeping people as
  connected as possible to their work groups or other routines,
  and eventually moving them from a focus on personal emotions to a focus on productive activities.

7

Toward Continuous Change

Staying Competitive through Change

Key Topics Covered in This Chapter

- *An explanation of continuous incremental change and its advantages*

- *How to determine whether people can handle continuous change*

- *Tips for implementing continuous incremental change in your workplace*

PREVIOUS chapters have treated change and change management as a onetime event. The company, having done its thing for many years, suddenly throws the cards in the air, everyone gets involved in reform and improvement, and then it's over. We call this "discontinuous change"—a single, abrupt shift from the past. The momentum of the organization is shifted, hopefully to a higher level of performance or in a more promising direction.

But the benefits of a successful single fix don't last forever. Change initiatives that accomplish stated goals often lead to complacency in senior management. Units that developed market-beating products and services during the change gradually shift their attention from innovation to defending their turf. Employees settle into routines and become more inward-looking. On top of all this, with each passing day, the environment of competition and technology is altered. This combination of complacency, defensive behavior, routines, inward focus, and ever-evolving competition is the enemy of progress; ultimately it creates a situation in which major reform is needed once again.

Continuous Incremental Change

If change programs are eventually followed by periods of organizational complacency and stasis—as described above—the alternative situation is one in which the organization and its people *continually* sense and respond to the external environment. Their radar is attuned to signals of change from customers, markets, competitors, and technologists. And they respond in appropriate ways. Simultaneously, they monitor internal activities to assure continuous improvement in key processes. Open communication assures that new ideas have a forum in which they are heard and objectively evaluated. Change is ongoing and takes place through many small steps—that is, through continuous incremental change, as illustrated in figure 7-1.

FIGURE 7 - 1

Discontinuous versus Continuous Incremental Change

Discontinuous change takes place through major, widely separated initiatives. Performance gains through those steps are followed by long periods of consolidation and quiescence.

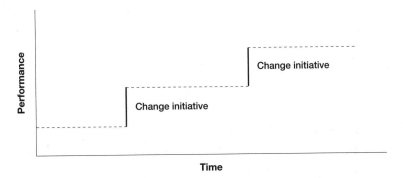

Continuous incremental change is made through a series of small but more frequent improvements.

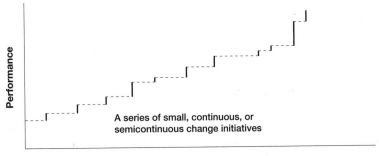

On the surface, the advantages of continuous incremental change are many:

- Small changes are easier to manage.

- Small changes enjoy greater probability of success than big ones.

- Disruption is short-term and confined to small units at any given time.

- The organization and its people are kept in a constant state of competitiveness and change-readiness.

Robert Schaffer, an author and management consultant, lent support for the advantages of incremental change when he wrote that "the larger the project, the greater the likelihood that the client organization lacks the requisite implementation skills, the managerial consensus, and the motivation necessary" to exploit the broad-ranging change initiative.[1]

Can People Handle It?

The critical question is, can managers manage and employees function in situations of continuous change? We know that too much change is mentally and physically disabling. People need anchors and a certain level of predictability in their lives in order to stay sane and healthy. Doctors, for example, tell us that a job loss or job change, a divorce or loss of a spouse, and a change of household address are all associated with subsequent illness and accidents. Combine two or more of these events and you might as well keep the phone number of the local ambulance service in your pocket. In this sense, too much change is downright unhealthy.

On the other hand, few people are strangers to changes in their work environments, from new technology and processes to new owners to the kinds of change initiatives described in previous chapters. The ability to change rapidly and frequently seems to be a critical mechanism for survival, and most people are able to handle it—particularly when nonwork aspects of their lives remain as stable anchors.

There is also some evidence of an "inoculation effect." Hurricane victims, for example, exhibit a "confidence curve" as a result of repeated crisis. Individuals who have been through one hurricane are the most stressed; they become hyper-watchful and tend to overprepare when they hear the next hurricane warning. In contrast, people who have had repeated exposures to hurricanes approach impending storms with greater equanimity. They know what preparation is required, and they expect that they'll come out of the hurricane in one piece.

If this analogy is transferable, participants in continuous change may exhibit a similar learning curve. The first big change initiative will shake them up and make them hypersensitive to the next one, but repeated exposures will inure them to change and make them psychologically better prepared to deal with it. However, this is only a hypothesis, and one that remains untested. And some speculate that the opposite could happen—that is, people exposed to repeated change could become more fragile, more resistant, and less equipped to manage successfully. The term "shell-shocked" comes to mind. Moreover, if someone experiences constant change, the question lingers as to whether she or he has dealt with the first change completely.

Given human differences, we can speculate that the human capacity to handle continuous change is tied to expectations. In some companies, people are routinely moved in and out of projects and positions; it is just the nature of work requirements in these organizations. But this is understood from the beginning and employees expect that there will be constant change. Indeed, some people are attracted to certain companies simply because they are fast-changing. If people know at the outset that frequent change—in positions, responsibilities, and the like—is part of the job, we can suppose that a kind of self-selection takes place. People who like that kind of experience will seek out jobs in these companies; and these companies will hire individuals who can accept frequent change.

The notion of continuous change as the ideal organizational state is fairly recent, so its long-term effects on individuals are not known. However, broad-based experience with continuous process improvement, primarily in Asia and less so in Europe and the United States, indicates that people can handle it. In Japan, continuous improvement is treated as routine, paradoxical as that may seem!

People should be able to handle regular change as long as it is:

- explained right;

- anticipated;

- handled in manageable doses;

- participatory rather than imposed; and

- made routine.

It also seems likely that such change is more likely to succeed and better for organizational health than the massive and disruptive change initiative that some corporations indulge in—usually when they are in near-death situations. In fact, continuous incremental change can save organizations from the *need* to adopt massive change initiatives. And such ongoing change can produce a cadre of managers and employees who have learned from repeated experience how to plan and implement change, making the overall organization more flexible and change-ready in the future.

Getting to Continuous Change

The following sections offer some tips on how to implement continuous incremental change in your organization and ensure that the effort succeeds.

Make Your Organization Change-Ready

As described in chapter 2, change-readiness is a function of:

- effective and respected leadership;

- employees who feel personally motivated to change; and

- an organization that is nonhierarchical and accustomed to collaborative work.

It is probably not a good idea to attempt continuous change if you're short on any one of these factors.

Conduct Continuous External Monitoring

The primary purpose of change is to array the organization's resources in ways that optimize its ability to deal with a shifting external environment. That means you have to understand what's going on in the outside world. Back in 1970, Harvard professor James Bright advocated that businesses conduct regular monitoring of external factors.[2] His advice was to:

- search the environment for signals of the forerunners of significant technological change;

- assume that the signals are based on substance, and identify possible consequences;

- determine which aspects of the environment should be observed and measured to verify the speed and direction of the new technology; and

- report the information in a timely manner.

Bright's aim was to provide companies with an early warning system capable of spotting technological developments and trajectories while there was still time to respond to them. This makes enormous sense if monitoring is conducted systematically, and if management has mechanisms for evaluating and acting on the blips that turn up on the radar screen.

There's also more to watch for than disruptive technological developments. It is also important to monitor changing customer requirements, human resource trends, and other critical aspects of business success.

Conduct Continuous Internal Monitoring

What Bright recommended for external scanning applies equally to internal operations. The focus here should be on key internal processes. Are they fast, flexible, and efficient? Every operating unit should have a team of people that provides regular oversight of the unit's key functions. The team should include people representing different levels and skills, and should be rotated regularly. Finding and fixing problems and weaknesses before they loom large is the best way to avoid costly and difficult change initiatives.

Provide Meaningful Anchors

No matter how prepared people are for regular change, they still need anchors—things that provide a sense of routine, familiarity, and continuity. As noted previously, too much change is unsettling and unhealthy. But what kinds of anchors are necessary? Years ago when he wrote *Future Shock,* author/futurist Alvin Toffler encouraged his readers to keep parts of their surroundings constant—even something as mundane as the style of clothing they liked to wear. Since the gods of fashion would change those styles, he suggested buying several pair of favorite shoes and other everyday items, and putting them on the shelf. When the current pair of shoes wore out, you'd have another pair handy, even though they had long disappeared from stores. Something similar may apply in the workplace.

First and foremost, remember that people are social animals and that work has a powerful social dimension. So think of ways to keep social linkages intact even as change is ongoing. Here are two suggestions:

- **Do what you can to keep healthy, functional work teams together.** In a broad-based study of U.S. workers, the Gallup Organization discovered that "having friends at work" is a key predictor of employee retention and satisfaction. Change programs that shuffle the personnel deck and isolate people from their workplace friends and acquaintances pay a big price in terms of low morale and defection. So avoid breaking up these relationships if you cannot make a solid business case for doing so.

- **Provide opportunities for social linkages at work.** Even if you must occasionally break up closely linked work groups, you can buffer the consequences by offering other opportunities for social interaction: a common lunchroom, a golfing league, and so forth. These bonds may replace the ones that your change program has broken elsewhere.

A second, higher-order anchoring opportunity is found in the purpose of the enterprise itself. James Collins and Jerry Porras, coauthors of the highly successful *Built to Last,* make the point that companies that enjoy enduring success—Hewlett-Packard, 3M, Johnson & Johnson, Sony, and others—have core values, core purposes, and ideologies that remain immutable over time, although their strategies, product lines, and operating practices are constantly adapting to a changing world. These core elements, they write, provide the glue that holds an organization together as it grows, decentralizes, diversifies, expands globally, and develops workplace diversity.[3]

What are your company's core values, core purposes, and ideologies? If they are strong, they can provide the anchors that people need to stay healthy and steady in fast-changing environments. (See "Core Values and Core Purpose" for more on this topic.)

Core Values and Core Purpose

Core values are a company's essential tenets. And they can be the secure anchor your people need to stay balanced and healthy in an environment of continuous change. Consider these examples:

Walt Disney

- No cynicism

- Creativity, dreams, and imagination

- Fanatical attention to consistency and detail

- Preservation and control of the Disney magic

Continued

Nordstrom

- Service to the customer above all else

- Hard work and individual productivity

- Never being satisfied

- Excellence in reputation; being part of something special

Core purpose is a company's reason for being. Here are some examples:

- 3M: To solve unsolved problems innovatively

- Cargill: To improve the standard of living around the world

- Hewlett-Packard: To make technical contributions for the advancement and welfare of humanity

- McKinsey & Company: To help leading corporations and governments be more successful

---

SOURCE: James C. Collins and Jerry I. Porras, "Building Your Company's Vision," *Harvard Business Review* 74, no. 5 (September–October 1996): 68–69.

Summing Up

This chapter discussed two different types of change:

- **Discontinuous change** was described as a single, abrupt shift from the past followed by a long period of stability, at which point another major change often needs to be made.

- **Continuous incremental change** is characterized by a series of small, discrete changes over a long period of time.

Continuous incremental change has certain advantages:

- Small changes are easier to manage, less disruptive, have a greater likelihood of success than larger ones, and can keep an organization on the cutting edge of competition.

- Repeated exposure may inure people to change and make them psychologically better prepared to deal with it.

Managers can move their organizations toward continuous incremental change by:

- making their organizations change-ready;

- conducting continuous internal and external monitoring; and

- providing people with meaningful anchors.

Useful Implementation Tools

This appendix contains four forms that you may find useful at various times during a change initiative. All are adapted from Harvard ManageMentor®, an online help source for subscribers. For interactive versions of these forms, please visit www.elearning.hbsp .org/businesstools. Here's a list of the diagnostic tests, checklists, and worksheets found in this appendix:

1. **Self–Evaluation: Characteristics of Effective Leadership.** Use this form to evaluate your own leadership capabilities. Change programs require leadership at all levels.

2. **Managing Stress Levels.** This checklist is a helpful tool for identifying and managing stress among the people you deal with.

3. **Focus and Synergy.** This checklist will help you identify obstacles encountered in the change process. Use this form or something like it to keep your team focused on the most important problems. For each obstacle to your team's progress, list and evaluate options for overcoming it. Also list any allies, additional resources, or special training your team members will need in order to collaborate most effectively on the chosen option.

4. **Gathering and Sharing Information.** This checklist can help you in the all–important business of communicating, which must be done regularly and through different channels during a change initiative. Use this form to collect and summarize the information your team needs to be effective and to change.

TABLE A - 1

Self-Evaluation: Characteristics of Effective Leadership

The questions below relate to characteristics of effective leaders. Use the questions to evaluate whether you possess these characteristics. Use the results to see where you might focus to strengthen your leadership skills.

Characteristics of Effective Leaders	Yes	No
Caring		
1. Do you empathize with other people's needs, concerns, and goals?		
2. Would staff members confirm that you show such empathy?		
Comfort with ambiguity		
3. Are you willing to take calculated risks?		
4. Are you comfortable with a certain level of disruption and conflict?		
Persistent; tenacious		
5. When pursuing a goal, do you maintain a positive, focused attitude, despite obstacles?		
Excellent communicators		
6. Do you listen closely (rather than have a response ready before the other person finishes)?		
7. Are you comfortable running meetings?		
8. Are you comfortable making presentations and speaking in public?		
9. Do you have the skills needed to negotiate in a variety of settings?		
Politically astute		
10. Could you diagram for yourself your organization's power structure?		
11. Can you articulate the concerns of your organization's most powerful groups?		
12. Can you identify those individuals within your organization that will support you when needed?		
13. Do you know where to turn for the resources you need?		
Able to use humor		
14. Do you know how to use humor to relieve tense or uncomfortable situations?		
Levelheaded		
15. In situations that are full of turmoil and confusion, do you stay calm and levelheaded?		

Characteristics of Effective Leaders	Yes	No
Self-aware		
16. Are you aware/can you describe how your own patterns of behavior impact others?		

If you answered "yes" to most of these questions, you have the characteristics of an effective leader.

If you answered "no" to some or many of these questions, you may want to consider how you can further develop these effective leadership characteristics.

Source: HMM Leading and Motivating.

TABLE A - 2

Managing Stress Levels

What bothers the individuals on your team the most about the current changes in your workplace? What are the sources of the stress?

How can you minimize or eliminate the excess stress?

____ Give advance warning, minimize surprises

____ Encourage the sharing of information

____ Foster a sense of humor in the workplace

____ Reassess/reassign work tasks to balance workloads

____ Recognize feelings and encourage members to express them

What sources of support (including peer or supervisory support) can you enlist to help manage stress levels?

List each member of your team. What are each member's prevailing emotions right now? Identify ways in which you can respond to each team member.

Team Member	Status/Symptoms	Ways to Respond

Source: HMM Capitalizing on Change.

TABLE A - 3

Focus and Synergy

Obstacle to Team's Progress	Options for Overcoming the Obstacle	Rank the Options (**1** most promising, **5** least promising)	Allies, Resources, Special Training

Source: HMM Capitalizing on Change.

TABLE A - 4

Gathering and Sharing Information

When was the last time you updated team members about the latest developments in the current change process? What were their specific concerns?

List the most significant new initiatives currently under way for the company as a whole, your division or unit, and your individual team.

What are the major rumors now running through the organization? What information about each can you share with your team?

What is the best way of making this information relevant to your team (e.g., one-on-one meeting, general meeting, memo)?

Development/Rumor/Initiative	Method	Timing

Source: HMM Capitalizing on Change.

How to Choose and Work with Consultants

The management consulting business has grown to be a multibillion dollar business, and it continues to grow. As a group—and despite a number of notable and controversial failures—consultants have much to offer. The problem for executives is how to know when their services are needed, whom to hire, and how to work with them successfully. What types of projects are best suited to outside consultants? How do you choose the most compatible consultant or firm? What level of service should you expect? And what are the keys to managing the relationship? This appendix, adapted from Tom Rodenhauser's article in *Harvard Management Update,* "How to Choose—and Work with—Consultants," can help you answer these questions.

When to Hire a Consultant

Generally, there are two reasons for hiring a consulting firm. One, there is a specific problem that needs addressing—for example, an antiquated bill-processing system needs to be overhauled—and you lack the internal expertise. Two, you are considering a strategic business issue—your company is thinking about expanding into Europe—and require outside, objective counsel. Consultants are, first and foremost, advisers. But their advice is no substitute for certain preliminary work that only you (or your company) can carry out. So, before considering hiring a consultant, ask yourself four questions:

1. **Do you understand the project's mission clearly?** Clients and consultants often have different views of the project's ultimate goal, and the objectives are often vaguely defined (for example, "improving a business process"). A consulting assignment without measurable targets usually results in disappointment. Before contacting consultants, spell out the scope and purpose of the proposed project.

2. **Does management fully support—organizationally and financially—the consultant's mission?** The disengagement of senior management from the consulting project guarantees failure. All too often, frontline managers advocate consulting services without the full support of higher-ups. Conversely, senior executives may foist their favorite consultants upon managers. The internal disconnect wastes time and money and breeds distrust, which can poison the project. Reach consensus on the need for outside counsel before going forward.

3. **When should the engagement end?** Consulting and outsourcing are two vastly different activities. Business process management, as outsourcing is euphemistically called, is a long-term contract between the company and an outside agent to handle a central business operation. Consulting assignments should have a definite beginning and end. It's unwise and ultimately unprofitable to hire management consultants to run the entire business, which is what happens with open-ended engagements.

4. **Can your company provide the necessary ongoing support after the project's completion?** Consulting is like exercise: without dedicated follow-up, it's wasted effort. To ensure continued success, monitor the post-consulting program closely.

Finding the Right Consultant

This is a daunting task for those unfamiliar with the industry. Some database and directory companies, such as Dun & Bradstreet and Gale Research, identify more than 200,000 U.S. consulting firms. An equal number can be found in Europe and Asia. These sources can be helpful in pinpointing consulting firms by the industries they serve, their geographic location, or the services they provide. Most large consultancies have offices in every major city and are thus easy to contact. Increasingly, smaller firms are advertising their services via Web sites or through such brokering services as The Expert Marketplace or the Management Consultant Network.

Once you've identified several likely candidates, request proposals from them. Consider proposals as the consultant's calling card. Never pay for a proposal or agree to a "handshake deal" for consulting services. And although there is no set formula for proposals, a well-crafted document will clearly and concisely answer the following:

- Does the consultant understand the problem?

- Are the approach and methodology for solving the problem clearly and succinctly presented?

- Are the benefits quantifiable?

- What are the consulting team's qualifications and experience?

- What are the fees?

Studying the proposal will give you a good feel for the firm's fit with your company. Jargon-filled proposals that don't define the end product are useless; you need to clearly understand what results will be delivered and by when.

Consultants rarely describe the specifics of their work to outsiders for fear of breaching client confidentiality. This makes in-depth reference checking difficult—but it is vital nonetheless. Ask finalists for the names and numbers of clients whose projects most closely match your own.

Fees

Most consulting services are billed on a per-diem basis; retainers are used for long-term projects. The fees may seem exorbitant on the surface, but good consulting is worth the price, particularly when results are clearly defined. Establishing clear measures for anticipated results takes time but is very important since the process itself allows the consultant and client to establish standards for performance. It also allows the client to attach a dollar value to the benefits while the consultant knows what he'll receive for the work involved.

How to Improve Your Chances of Success

Referrals are probably the most reliable indicators of a consultancy's fit with your company and its specific needs, and that fit is very important. Moreover, many consulting assignments fail when clients abdicate their responsibility to actively participate in programs in which consultants have either a leadership or partnership role. Consultants are not miracle workers, and clients aren't helpless—each is responsible for ensuring that an engagement achieves the desired result.

Questions to Ask before Signing Up a Consulting Firm

- What assignments has your firm conducted that are similar to ours?

- Who would be the lead consultant in the engagement, and what in his background would make him the right person for the job?

- Who would the other team members be, and what do they bring to the table?

- Can you provide a detailed breakdown of fees, including cost of team members, clerical work, and out-of-pocket expenses?

- Will you do a post-engagement audit?

- Can you specify deliverables?

- What operational gains should we expect you to produce?

- Does your firm guarantee its work?

In addition to these questions, it is also important to consider the candidate firm's reputation in the business community, and in your industry in particular.

Notes

Chapter 1

1. Michael Beer and Nitin Nohria, "Cracking the Code of Change," *Harvard Business Review* 78, no. 3 (May–June 2000): 133–141.

2. American Management Association, "1993 Survey on Downsizing," (New York: American Management Association, 1993), 3.

3. Beer and Nohria, "Cracking the Code of Change," 134–135.

4. Dave Ulrich, *Human Resource Champions* (Boston: Harvard Business School Press, 1996), 153.

Chapter 2

1. Beth Axelrod, Helen Handfield-Jones, and Ed Michaels, "A New Game for C Players," *Harvard Business Review* 80, no. 1 (January 2002): 83.

2. Richard Luecke, *Scuttle Your Ships Before Advancing* (New York: Oxford University Press, 1994), 73.

3. For a fascinating account of GM's slow awakening to its quality problems, see Gregory H. Watson, *Strategic Benchmarking* (New York: John Wiley & Sons, Inc., 1993), 129–143.

4. Michael Beer, "Leading Change," Class note 9-488-037 (Boston: Harvard Business School, 1988, revised 1991), 2.

5. Edward E. Lawler III, "Pay System Change: Lag, Lead, or Both?" in *Breaking the Code of Change,* eds. Michael Beer and Nitin Nohria (Boston, MA: Harvard Business School Press, 2000), 323–336.

6. Richard Axelrod, "Democratic Approaches to Change Make a Big Difference in Turbulent Times," *Harvard Management Update,* November 2001, 3.

7. Gregory H. Watson, *Strategic Benchmarking* (New York: John Wiley & Sons, Inc., 1993), 131.

Chapter 3

1. Michael Beer and Nitin Nohria, "Cracking the Code of Change," *Harvard Business Review* 78, no. 3 (May–June 2000): 133–141.

2. "How to Get Aboard a Major Change Effort: An Interview with John Kotter," *Harvard Management Update,* September 1996.

3. Michael Beer, Russell A. Eisenstat, and Bert Spector, "Why Change Programs Don't Produce Change," *Harvard Business Review* 68, no. 6 (November–December 1990): 7–12.

4. Ibid.

5. John P. Kotter, "Leading Change: Why Transformation Efforts Fail," *Harvard Business Review* 73, no. 2 (March–April 1995): 59–67.

6. Paul Strebel, "Why Do Employees Resist Change?" *Harvard Business Review* 74, no. 3 (May–June 1996): 86–92.

7. Adapted from *Realizing Change,* an interactive CD-ROM based on the change literature of John Kotter (Boston, MA: Harvard Business School Publishing, 1997).

8. Michael Beer, Russell A. Eisenstat, and Bert Spector, *The Critical Path to Corporate Renewal* (Boston, MA: Harvard Business School Press, 1990), 184–201.

9. Ibid., 202.

10. Robert H. Schaffer and Harvey A. Thomson, "Successful Change Programs Begin with Results," *Harvard Business Review* 70, no. 1 (January–February 1992): 80–89.

11. The SQA story is told in David Bovet and Joseph Martha, *Value Nets* (New York: John Wiley & Sons, Inc., 2000), 169–182.

12. Everett M. Rogers, *Diffusion of Innovation,* 3rd edition (New York: The Free Press, 1983), 5.

Chapter 4

1. Larry Alexander, "Successfully Implementing Strategic Decisions," *Long Range Planning* 18, no. 3 (1985): 91–97.

2. Michael L. Tushman and Charles A. O'Reilly III, *Winning through Innovation* (Boston, MA: Harvard Business School Press, 1997), 190.

3. John F. Kotter, *Leading Change* (Boston, MA: Harvard Business School Press, 1996).

4. This section leans heavily on Todd Jick, "Implementing Change," Class note 9-491-114 (Boston: Harvard Business School, 1991).

5. John Kotter, "Leading Change: Why Transformation Efforts Fail," *Harvard Business Review* 73, no. 2 (March–April 1995): 66.

6. Adapted from Rebecca Saunders, "Communicating Change," *Harvard Management Communication Letter,* August 1999.

7. Michael Beer and Nitin Nohria, "Cracking the Code of Change," *Harvard Business Review* 78, no. 3 (May–June 2000): 137.

Chapter 5

1. Eric Hoffer, *The Ordeal of Change* (Cutchogue, NY: Buccaneer Books, 1976), 3.

2. See the Myers-Briggs Type Indicator®, Consulting Psychologists Press, Inc.

3. See W. Christopher Musselwhite and Robyn Ingram, *Change Style Indicator* (Greensboro, NC: The Discovery Learning Press, 1999).

4. Ibid., 4.

5. Paul R. Lawrence, "How to Deal With Resistance to Change," *Harvard Business Review* XLVII (January–February 1969): 4–12, 166–176.

6. Robert Kegan and Lisa Laskow Lahey, "The Real Reason People Won't Change," *Harvard Business Review* 79, no. 10 (November 2001): 84–92.

7. Everett M. Rogers, *Diffusion of Innovation,* 3rd ed. (New York: The Free Press, 1983) 315–316.

Chapter 6

1. Harry Woodward and Steve Bucholz, *Aftershock* (New York: John Wiley & Sons, Inc., 1987).

2. Adapted from Todd D. Jick, "Note on the Recipients of Change," Note 9-491-039 (Boston: Harvard Business School, 1990, revised 1996).

3. Ken Hultmans, *The Path of Least Resistance* (Austin, TX: Learning Concepts, 1979).

Chapter 7

1. Robert Schaffer, "Rapid-Cycle Successes versus the Titanics," in *Breaking the Code of Change,* eds. Michael Beer and Nitin Nohria (Boston, MA: Harvard Business School Press, 2000), 362.

2. James R. Bright, "Evaluating Signals of Technological Change," *Harvard Business Review* XLVIII (January–February 1970): 64.

3. James C. Collins and Jerry I. Porras, "Building Your Company's Vision," *Harvard Business Review* 74, no. 5 (September–October 1996): 66.

For Further Reading

Communication Issues

Larkin, T. J., and Sandar Larkin. "Reaching and Changing Frontline Employees," *Harvard Business Review* 74, no. 3 (May–June 1996): 95–104. Planning a major change in your organization? If so, chances are you have arranged a huge rally, rousing speeches, videos, and special editions of the company paper. Stop. This sort of communication does not work. If you want people to change the way they do their jobs, you must change the way you communicate with them. Drawing on their own research and the research of other communication experts from the past two decades, the authors argue that senior managers—and most communication consultants—have refused to hear what frontline workers have been trying to tell them: When you need to communicate a major change, spend most of your time, money, and effort on frontline supervisors.

General Issues

Beer, Michael, Russell A. Eisenstat, and Bert Spector. *The Critical Path to Corporate Renewal*. Boston, MA: Harvard Business School Press, 1990. Based on a study of six large corporations that tried to transform themselves, this book explains why some enjoyed greater success than others, and offers a practical approach that managers can adopt. Also worth reading from these same authors is, "Why Change Programs Don't Produce Change," *Harvard Business Review* 68, no. 6 (November–December 1990): 7–12.

Brenneman, Greg. "Right Away and All at Once: How We Saved Continental," *Harvard Business Review* 76, no. 5 (September–October 1998): 162–179. Not many corporatewide change programs succeed. This one did, and it makes for interesting reading. In 1994, Continental Airlines was headed for a crash landing—quickly running out of customers and cash. A simple strategy, executed fast, right away, and all at once, says Greg Brenneman, president and COO of the company, pulled it out of its death spiral. He describes the five lessons he learned during this dramatic turnaround. With Gordon Bethune, Continental's chairman and CEO, Brenneman devised the Go Forward Plan, a straightforward strategy focused on four key elements: understanding the market, increasing revenues, improving the product, and transforming the corporate culture. Brenneman admits that the plan wasn't complicated—it was pure common sense. The tough part was getting it done. "Do it now!" became the rallying cry of the movement, and the power of momentum carried Continental to success.

Kotter, John P. *Leading Change*. Boston: Harvard Business School Press, 1996. Emphasizing the need for leadership to make change happen—and stick—this book identifies an eight-step process that every organization must go through in order to achieve change goals. It shows where and how people often derail the process, and how those errors can be avoided.

Realizing Change (part of The Interactive Manager Series of multimedia learning tools on CD-ROM). Boston: Harvard Business School Publishing, 1999. *Realizing Change,* based on John Kotter's book, *Leading Change,* is designed to help managers acquire the understanding and skills needed to lead and manage organizational change. Unlike the book, the CD version organizes the change agenda into three sequential phases: set up, roll out, and follow through. The interactive nature of the program allows users to drill down into various levels of detail on each phase, including case studies and other available readings.

Schaffer, Robert H., and Harvey A. Thomson. "Successful Change Programs Begin with Results," *Harvard Business Review* 70, no. 1 (January–February 1992): 80–89. If you think that big change programs with grandiose visions are bunk, you'll like this article. Most corporate improvement efforts have negligible results, according to these authors, because they focus on activities, not results, and there is no explicit connection between action and outcome. "Results-driven" approaches offer greater potential for improvement because they focus on achieving specific, measurable goals. By committing to incremental change, managers not only can see results faster but also determine more quickly what is working and what isn't.

Leadership Issues

Conner, Daryl R. *Managing at the Speed of Change: How Resilient Managers Succeed and Prosper Where Others Fail*. New York: Villard Books, 1993. The author notes eight patterns and many principles that can be used successfully by those responsible for change in their organizations. The patterns involve the nature of change, the process of change, the roles played during change, resistance to change, commitment to change, how change affects culture, synergism, and the nature of resilience. Connor states that the degree to which people demonstrate resilience is the key factor in managing change successfully.

Luecke, Richard. *Scuttle Your Ships Before Advancing: And Other Lessons from History on Leadership and Change for Today's Managers.* New York: Oxford University Press, 1994. This collection of historical episodes dramatizes the plight of leaders faced with uncertainty and change. The episodes range from the Aztec world at the time of Cortez's appearance, to the battle of Agincourt, to revolutionary Boston. Among other things, the book contains an interesting chapter on the power of ideas to drive change.

People Issues

Jeffreys, J. Shep. *Coping with Workplace Change: Dealing with Loss and Grief.* Menlo Park, CA: Crisp Publications, 1995. This short book was written for survivors of layoffs and other organizational changes, but it holds value for anyone in an organization undergoing major change.

Musselwhite, W. Christopher, and Robyn Ingram. *Change Style Indicator.* Greensboro, NC: The Discovery Learning Press, 1999. This "Study Guide" is an assessment instrument designed to measure an individual's preferred style in approaching change and in addressing situations involving change. Knowing in advance how people respond to change can help you enlist their collaboration. This and Discovery Learning's other training and consulting products are available through its Web site: <http://www.discoverylearning.com>.

Pritchett, Price. *New Work Habits for a Radically Changing World.* Dallas, TX: Pritchett & Associates, 1994. This book offers guidelines for job management during radical change. The author's viewpoint is that change in organizations is only a response to change in the world, and therefore, employees must take personal responsibility for their own careers.

Strebel, Paul. "Why Do Employees Resist Change?" *Harvard Business Review* 74, no. 3 (May–June 1996): 86–92. The problem with many change programs isn't the programs themselves. It's that too few people, at every level, really support the initiative with their hearts and minds. This interesting article explains that organizations have personal compacts with their employees. Change efforts fail when those compacts are ignored.

Index

agents, change. *See* change agents

Brenneman, Greg, 62–63

Champion International, 12–13
change
  continuous (*see* continuous
    change)
  economic approach (*see* Theory E)
  implementing (*see* implementing
    change)
  organizational capabilities
    approach (*see* Theory O)
  process of (*see* seven steps to
    change)
  readiness for (*see* change-readiness)
  summary, 15
  types of, 8–9
change agents
  identifying, 78, 79
  insider-outsider, 78, 79–80
  roles of, 77
change-readiness
  achieving, 25–29
  approaches for accomplishing
    change, 21–22
  complacency signs, 21–22, 23*t*
  leadership and, 18–19

motivation to change, 19–21
nonhierarchical organizations
  and, 24–25
rewards as motivation, 22–24
summary, 29–30
conservers and change, 72, 73
consultants and implementing
  change
  background to use, 62, 64
  choosing, 120–121, 123
  fees, 121–122
  success of partnership, 122
  types and approaches used,
    64–65
  variations in roles, 65–67
  when to hire, 119–120
Continental Airlines, 62–63
continuous change
  accomplishing, 106, 107–109,
    110
  advantages of, 104
  discontinuous versus, 102–104
  information management
    evaluation, 118*t*
  peoples' responses to, 104–106
  summary, 110–111
C performers, 19

Deming, W. Edwards, 19–20

economic approach to change.
    See Theory E
Eddystone Generating Station,
    40–42
empowering people, 26–27, 28
Endurance, 98–99

Ford Motor Company, 20–21

General Electric, 13–15, 66
General Motors, 21, 29

Herman Miller Company, 43
HR personnel, 46–47
human factors regarding change.
    See social and human factors;
    stress due to workplace change

implementing change
    common problems, 52–53
    communication's importance,
        62–63
    communication tips, 60–62
    consistency need, 56–57
    consultants and (*see* consultants
        and implementing change)
    enabling structures development,
        57–58
    leadership self-evaluation,
        114–115*t*
    milestone celebration, 58–59
    obstacles identification, 117*t*
    online tools Web site, 113
    plan creation, 54–56
    stress levels management
        evaluation, 116*t*
    summary, 67–68
    team member selection, 53–54, 55

leadership
    change-readiness and, 18–19
    in a change situation, example
        of, 98–99
    characteristics of change leaders,
        38–39
    relationship to management, 46,
        47*f*
    self-evaluation, 114–115*t*

managers' role in change
    dealing with change, 88–89
    helping employees, 94–95, 96
    role in steps to change, 46–47

Nordstrom, 110

organizational capabilities approach
        to change. *See* Theory O
originators and change, 72, 73–74

passive resisters and change, 76
pragmatists and change, 72, 73

resisters
    social factors regarding change
        and, 74–76
    stress due to change and, 96–97
rewards
    change implementation and,
        58, 59
    change-readiness and, 22–24

Scott Paper, 12–13
seven steps to change
    focus on results, 39–42, 117*t*

institutionalizing of success, 44
leaders' and managers' roles,
     46–47
leadership and, 38–39
mistakes to avoid, 47–48
motivating change, 37
problem identification, 33–35
self-diagnosis of approach, 45*t*
shared vision development,
     36–38
solution development, 35–36
start at periphery, 43–44
strategy monitoring and adjust-
     ment, 45
summary, 49–50
Shackleton, Sir Ernest, 98–99
"simple, quick, affordable" (SQA),
     43
social and human factors
     change agents, 77, 78, 79–80
     rank and file reactions, 70–74
     resisters, 74–76
     stress caused by change (*see* stress
          due to workplace change)
     summary, 81
statistical process control (SPC),
     19–21
stress due to workplace change
     individual's role in dealing with
          change, 89–92

leadership example, 98–99
managers' role in dealing with
     change, 88–89
managers' role in helping employ-
     ees, 92–96
resisters and, 96–97
sense of loss and anxiety, 85–86
stages of reactions, 86–88
stress levels management evalua-
     tion, 116*t*
summary, 99–100

Theory E
     described, 10, 65–66
     theories comparison, 11–15, 15*t*
Theory O
     described, 11, 66
     theories comparison, 11–15, 15*t*

Walt Disney, 109
Web site for online change tools,
     113

Xerox, 37

About the Subject Adviser

MIKE BEER is Cahners-Rabb Professor of Business Administration, Emeritus, at the Harvard Business School, where he still teaches in the areas of organizational effectiveness, human resource management, and organizational change. Prior to joining the Harvard faculty, he was Director of Organization Research and Development at Corning, Inc., where he was responsible for stimulating a number of innovations in management. He has authored or coauthored several books and articles. *The Critical Path to Corporate Renewal* (Harvard Business School Press, 1990), which deals with the problems of large-scale corporate change, won the Johnson, Smith, and Knisley Award for the best book in executive leadership in 1991 and was a finalist for the Academy of Management Terry Book Award that year. His most recent book, edited with Nitin Nohria, is *Breaking the Code of Change* (Harvard Business School Press, 2000). In the last several years, Professor Beer has developed and researched a process by which top teams can assess and develop their organization's capability to implement their strategy. He has served on the editorial board of several journals and the board of governors of the Academy of Management, is Chairman of the Center for Organizational Fitness, and has consulted with many Fortune 500 companies.

About the Writer

RICHARD LUECKE is the writer of several books in the Harvard Business Essentials series. Based in Salem, Massachusetts, Mr. Luecke has authored or developed over thirty books and dozens of articles on a wide range of business subjects. He has an M.B.A. from the University of St. Thomas.

Need smart, actionable management advice?

Look no further than your desktop.

Harvard ManageMentor®, a popular online performance support tool from Harvard Business School Publishing, brings how-to guidance and advice to your desktop, ready when you need it, on a host of issues critical to your work.

Heading up a new team? Resolving a conflict between employees? Preparing a make-or-break presentation for a client? Setting next year's budget? Harvard ManageMentor®Online delivers answers and advice on 33 topics right to your desktop—any time, all the time, just in time.

- Downloadable modules on 28 essential topics allow you to build a personal management resource center right on your computer

- Practical tips, tools, checklists, and resources help you enhance productivity and performance now

- Advice from seasoned experts in finance, communications, teamwork, coaching and more—accessible with a few mouse clicks

- Multiple language versions available

Go to **http://www.harvardmanagementor.com/demo** today to try out two complimentary Harvard ManageMentor® (HMM) Online topics.

Individual topic modules are available for $14.95 each, or you can order the complete HMM Online program (33 topics in all) for $129. Corporate site licenses are also available. For more information or to order, call 800.795.5200 (outside the U.S. and Canada: 617.783.7888) or visit www.harvardmanagementor.com/demo.

HARVARD
ManageMentor®
An online resource for
managers in a hurry